EVERYONE'S
A COACH

OTHER BOOKS BY THE AUTHORS

Don Shula

The Winning Edge
   (with Lou Sahadi)

Ken Blanchard

We Are the Beloved

The One Minute Manager
   (with Spencer Johnson)

Management of Organizational Behavior
   (with Paul Hersey) 6th edition

The Power of Ethical Management
   (with Norman Vincent Peale)

Raving Fans
   (with Sheldon Bowles)

Putting the One Minute Manager to Work
   (with Robert Lorber)

Leadership and the One Minute Manager
   (with Drea Zigarmi and Patricia Zigarmi)

The One Minute Manager Builds High Performing Teams
   (with Don Carew and Eunice Parisi-Carew)

The One Minute Manager Meets the Monkey
   (with William Oncken and Hal Burrows)

The One Minute Manager Gets Fit
   (with D. W. Edington and Marjorie Blanchard)

Playing the Great Game of Golf

DON SHULA & KEN BLANCHARD

EVERYONE'S A COACH

You Can Inspire Anyone to Be a Winner

HarperBusiness
New York, New York

ZondervanPublishingHouse
Grand Rapids, Michigan

Everyone's a Coach
Copyright © 1995 by Shula Enterprises and Blanchard Family Partnership

Co-published by ZondervanPublishingHouse and HarperBusiness, divisions of HarperCollins*Publishers*.

Requests for information should be addressed to:
Zondervan Publishing House
Grand Rapids, Michigan 49530

Library of Congress Cataloging-in-Publication Data

Shula, Don, 1930–
    Everyone's a coach : you can inspire anyone to be a winner / Don Shula and Ken Blanchard.
       p.   m.
    ISBN 0-310-50120-2 (alk. paper)
    1. Football—Coaching—Philosophy. 2. Achievement motivation. 3. Motivation (Psychology) 4. Leadership.   I. Blanchard, Kenneth H. II. Title.
GV954.4.S56   1995
796.332'07'7—dc20   95–33423
                                                                 CIP

Edited by Lyn Cryderman
Interior design by Sue Koppenol

Printed in the United States of America

95 96 97 98 99 00 01 02/❖ DH/ 10 9 8 7 6 5 4 3 2 1

This edition printed on acid-free paper and meets the American National Standards Institute Z39.48 standard.

■   *To Mary Anne Shula and Margie Blanchard*
    for their constant love, support, encouragement,
    and helpful wisdom throughout the writing of this book.

CONTENTS

ACKNOWLEDGMENTS

SPECIAL THANKS TO:

Charlie Morgan, for seeing the potential power of our partnership and persisting until we sat down together and began this project. He then supported us at every turn. Charlie is the inspiration behind this book.

Jim Ballard, for his writing support, creativity, and commitment to this project. After the first draft, Jim became Ken's writing partner. Eighteen-hour days writing, creating, and praying together were not unusual. Jim is not only a fabulous writer, but he is a warm and caring human being. This project soared in quality because of his contribution, and the ongoing guidance of the Big Four.

ONE-MINUTE PRAISINGS TO:

Margret McBride, our literary agent, who was excited about this project right from the beginning, and transferred that enthusiasm to our Harper Business/Zondervan publishing partners. Margret was always there with a smile, a good idea, and the willingness to follow up and make things happen.

Lyn Cryderman from Zondervan and *Adrian Zackheim* from Harper Business, our editors, for believing in us and this project, and for their insightful feedback that helped lift the book to continually higher levels.

Eleanor Terndrup, who has typed and nurtured Ken's books for over fifteen years. She was always there when Ken and Jim needed her—assisted by *David Witt*, one of the great utility resources of all time, who was ready to take a hand-off and run with the ball.

Scott DeGarmo, editor in chief of *Success* magazine, and *Lisa Berkowitz*, director of publicity for Harper Business, for believing in this book and creating some wonderful publicity events.

Dana Kyle, Harry Paul, and *Pete Psichogios,* Ken's strategic team, for planning, strategizing, and implementing the launch of this book.

Peggy Stanton, Lou Sahadi, and the sports staff of the *Miami Herald,* fine writers who have previously written about Don Shula and his philosophy toward football and life, for providing valuable information for this book.

And finally, to *Paul Hersey, Spencer Johnson, Robert Lorber* and *Norman Vincent Peale,* former co-authors with Ken, and *Gerald Nelson,* the originator of the One Minute Scolding, for influencing Ken's thinking and many of the concepts he presents in this book. ■

INTRODUCTION

SHULA

Football has been my way of life ever since I can remember. I love it. I love to compete. I love working with the team. When my classmates went off to careers in business, I stayed with football, first as a player, then as a coach. Over the past forty years I have played with and coached literally thousands of players, many of them now retired and enjoying a far more restful life than I. Over these years, football has brought home the crushing lows of defeat, but at other times, the ecstatic highs of achievement. Looking back, I wouldn't trade it for anything.

The game of football hasn't really changed much over the years. Today we have more sophisticated offensive and defensive schemes, special teams, strength training, and better training facilities. But the objective is essentially the same: put a cohesive unit on the field that's able to drive the ball down the field and put points on the scoreboard and stop the other team from scoring. Simple, isn't it? For more than thirty years, my life has been structured to lead teams to do that. I'm just a guy who rolls up his sleeves every day and works hard to get the best out of his team. Every week is a carbon copy of the prior week. Only the faces and jerseys change—and the game plan to face the new opponent.

Most of you reading this book are not football coaches and never will be. But whether you're a teacher or a committee chairman, a sales manager or a choir leader, a Little League coach or a military officer, you can improve your ability to get the best performance from people. The principles I've used successfully in coaching the Baltimore Colts and the Miami Dolphins for over three decades can help you do that.

Over the years, I've focused my efforts on helping players and coaches. I hadn't thought much about passing along to others what I've learned in my years of NFL coaching (except maybe to my coaching staff who are trying to help us win a Super Bowl). But when Ken and I met and discussed doing a project together that would help executives, coaches, teachers, or parents—anyone who is in a position to bring out the best in people—it made sense to me. Football and business are different, of course; but these days, I think the challenge for business people is not that different from what I face. The competition is fierce. The strategizing is similar; finding and using that edge that makes the difference requires constant attention. Then there are people; they come to you with skills and talents; your job is to instruct, discipline, and inspire them to do things better than they thought they could do them on their own.

In the end, whether it's sports or business, winning and losing doesn't depend on trick plays or using new systems each week. The information your competition has is not that different from yours. So what are you going to use to win? It comes down to a matter of motivating people to work hard and prepare to play as a team. That's what really counts. In a word, it's coaching.

What makes a great coach? That's a question I've been asked many times over the years. This book contains my answer. Of course, no book can give you the thing that drives all real success—passion and enthusiasm for what you do. How do you get this burning in the gut, this desire to win that won't quit? I don't know. But with it the advice in this book can give you some valuable tools to be the best.

—Miami, Spring 1995

BLANCHARD

My life is not centered around football but around leadership. For the last thirty years, I've studied people and what contributes to effective behavior in organizations. I've acted as a coach for executives and managers who lead organizations. When I coauthored *The One Minute Manager,* I was amazed at the response that business leaders made to the simple, straightforward approach of the legendary character in the story. At that point, I began a search for simple truths to help leaders and managers be their best. That's why I was so fascinated when I met Don Shula in the spring of 1992 at the Dolphins training camp. Don impressed me as one of the most focused human beings I'd ever encountered. As I walked into his office, he greeted me by saying, "Nice to meet you. Unfortunately, I only have about ten minutes." Right away I knew I had met another One Minute Manager.

As it turned out, our meeting lasted about an hour, but since it was five days before the start of the college draft, Shula's mind was clearly on his team and on the kind of players they needed to be competitive in the next season. But the meeting had piqued my interest in Shula and the Miami Dolphins. I wondered:

- What makes this man tick?
- What drives him to coach year after year, when other coaches burn out and quit?
- What are the secrets of his personal game plan that have made him so successful over three decades in an ever-changing National Football League?
- How can these principles be communicated to others so they can help their teams and organizations succeed?

The last question intrigued me the most. Leaders come and go on the American landscape. There aren't many examples of people who have sustained success in their organizations over a long period of time in this kind of pressure-cooker environment, where evaluation is going on week by week. Somehow Don Shula has been able to do it. With my list of questions in mind, I began a learning quest—talking to Shula, visiting the Dolphins in their training camp, interviewing players and coaches and officials who knew and had worked with Don. As I began to gather my notes and to develop applications of Shula's coaching principles to the workplace, I came to the conclusion that all organizations are moving closer to what Shula and top football coaches face in their jobs.

Between 1945 and 1980 there was no competition in American business, domestically or in the foreign market. Back then even if some individual or department was falling down on the job, the organization—whether it was a school, the military, or the government—was still in business. If you were loyal to the organization, you were guaranteed job security.

Starting in 1980, the whole game began to change, and in the 1990s business is closer to football than ever before—especially in terms of how often your performance gets evaluated. I recently heard a manager tell an audience that he'd worked for his company for twenty-two years. He said, "I actually should tell you I've worked for my company for eighty-eight quarters. The way things are going, pretty soon I'll be telling you I've worked for them for twenty-two times fifty-two. Organizations today are under the gun almost every single week." Today there are no guarantees. If your organization doesn't take care of your customers and perform well, there's somebody out there who will. The pressure is on for people to perform at their best, so there has never been a greater need for effective coaching. Everybody's a coach in some aspect of life, and that means you. Regardless of whether you have an official title, there are people out there who need your help.

The message of this book is for anyone with the task of helping others perform better. No matter how good you are at coaching others, you can improve your ability. In writing this book, Don and I have used a tag-team format. First, he will share his secrets of successful coaching. Then I will seek to apply these same principles to your world. So grab your whistle and clipboard, and let's get in the game.

—San Diego, Spring 1995

When I took over the Dolphins in 1970, the press wanted to know what my three- or five-year plan was. I told them my plan was day-to-day.

■ DON SHULA

SHULA

I never set out to break George Halas's all-time coaching record of 324 wins. Naturally, I was proud when I surpassed it in the 1993 season, but the truth is, I never worry about win totals. They're a by-product of hard work—of doing our best every day, every week, every year. How long have I been coaching like this? Right from the beginning. From the moment I started coaching the Miami Dolphins in 1970, my day-to-day plan was very specific. I wanted to make sure we came out of every meeting a little more intelligent than when we went in, that we came off the practice field a little better prepared mentally and physically to play the game than we were before practice. I wanted us to make the most out of every meeting, every practice, and every preseason game to get us ready for the regular season.

My goals are the same every year. First of all, I want my team to qualify for the play-offs. Secondly, I want us to win the play-offs and get into the Super Bowl. And finally, I want to win the Super Bowl, which is symbolic of the world championship. If I had my way, we'd win every football game. That goal was far from everybody's mind, however, when I took over the Dolphins in 1970. The year before, their record was 3–8–1. Our first pre-season was cut short by a strike. When the team finally got to practice, I presented to the squad a plan that would make the most of every waking minute to get us ready to play football. We would have four workouts a day, following this schedule:

7:00 A.M.	PRACTICE 1: Work on special teams and kicking game
7:45	Breakfast

9:30	Meeting to cover morning practice points
10:00	PRACTICE 2: Work on running game—both offense and defense
11:30	Lunch
3:00 P.M.	Meeting to cover afternoon practice points
3:30	PRACTICE 3: Work on passing game—both offense and defense
6:00	Dinner
7:30	PRACTICE 4: Work until dark on making corrections
9:30	Meeting
10:30	Dismiss

My players couldn't believe what I was asking them to do. There was a lot of moaning and groaning from the guys. "Four practices a day!" "This is unheard of." "What's he trying to do? Kill us?" But also a few laughs. "All we're doing is dressing and undressing. What are we, ballplayers or strippers?"

When we won our first preseason game, there was less complaining. After we'd won a few more preseason games, and the press asked the players the reason for the turnaround, they all attributed it to the hard work we'd done to get ourselves ready to compete. The things they had complained the most about they later credited for the change in the football team. Incidentally, we went on to win ten games that season and were in the Super Bowl the next season.

What has produced winning football teams for us over the years has been our willingness to create practice systems and procedures that are aligned with our vision of perfection: *We want to win them all.* Everything I do is to prepare people to perform to the best of their ability. And you do that one day at a time.

BLANCHARD

Today's leading organizations share a commitment to constant improvement. They believe they're going to be better tomorrow than they were yesterday, better next week than last week, better next month than last month, and better next year than last year. To make that happen, you have to overcome people's inertia and resistance. Few people want to be pushed, but they need to be. I've learned that from Don Shula, who—like the late Norman Vincent Peale—came along at the perfect time in my life. Norman showed up when I was groping with my own spirituality. Who I am today was greatly influenced by the two years I spent with Norman working on our book *The Power of Ethical Management.* These past few years, I've started to confront my own behavior as an organizational leader. In its first fifteen years, our company, Blanchard Training and Development, Inc. (BTD), grew from a mom-and-pop organization—dependent on my wife, Margie, me, and some associates doing the training, to an international firm that produces and distributes learning materials and helps organizations change successfully. The pace of growth has been brisk, but at the same time leisurely. In that mode of operating I could play the part of a warm, fuzzy bear who always made everyone happy. Then suddenly, like many other organizations, we were confronted with a changing business environment. We had to abandon the comfort zone of the way we'd always done business. What to do? Enter Don Shula.

As I began to work with Shula, my attention at first was on collecting anecdotes, outlining, writing, and editing. Slowly I began to realize that Shula's energy was rubbing off on me. His one-pointed attention to detail, his commitment to getting it right, his ferocious incentive to make his team the best spoke to me. Don made me realize that if you're going to compete today and be the best, you have to push yourself and others—hard. At a recent company meeting, people were amazed (but applauded) when I said, "If you don't grow, you go!" and pointed the finger at myself to symbolize, "We all have to strive to continually get better." I committed "the new BTD" to serve our customers in such a way that we'd be in the human resource development Super Bowl. I told people it wasn't going to happen overnight. It would require us to go at it every day, every week, every year—sound familiar?

Not everyone was thrilled with my message. Have you had a similar experience when setting boundaries for children or pushing them to do what's required? When you make them work hard or do something they don't want to do, they don't like it. Most kids, however, come to feel later on that what you did made an important and valued difference in their lives. The other day, my mom and I were laughing about our recollection of times when I was growing up when she insisted my sister Sandy and I live up to her values and standards. (My mom is ninety-one years old and still as feisty as ever.) Sometimes when my sister and I wouldn't be permitted to go somewhere, we'd whine, "How come we can't go when all our friends are going?" She'd shout back, "Because their name isn't Blanchard!"

It doesn't take the Dolphin players long to realize that their coach's name is Shula and that he knows something important: if you allow sloppy practice and don't push your team to continually improve, sloppiness becomes a habit; then it's tougher to get the team to focus on getting better when it most needs to. Can you imagine the Dolphins say-

You have to respect Coach Shula's thirty years of excellence. That's no accident. You're a damn fool if you think so.

■ JOE GREENE,
DEFENSIVE LINE COACH, MIAMI DOLPHINS;
HALL OF FAME PLAYER, PITTSBURGH STEELERS

ing, "How come we have to practice so hard? The team that's in last place never practices like this!" As Shula says, the best way to continue to improve is to practice hard all the time.

C.O.A.C.H. TO *WIN*

Now that you've begun to learn about the secrets of Don Shula's success, we want to help you put the secrets into action on a day-to-day basis. We've organized the key points of the book into a simple acronym: C.O.A.C.H. Each letter stands for one of the five secrets of effective coaching, combining what Shula has been practicing and Blanchard has been teaching for over three decades.

Conviction-Driven

Effective leaders stand for something.

Overlearning

Effective leaders help their teams achieve practice perfection.

Audible-Ready

Effective leaders, and the people and teams they coach, are ready to change their game plan when the situation demands it.

Consistency

Effective leaders are predictable in their response to performance.

Honesty-Based

Effective leaders have high integrity and are clear and straightforward in their interactions with others.

SECRET #1

CONVICTION-DRIVEN

Being conviction-driven *means doing the right things for the right reasons. Beliefs and convictions provide the boundaries and direction that people want and need in order to perform well. Shula's conviction-driven leadership is based on his vision of perfection, his perspective on winning and losing, and his belief in leading by example, valuing respect more than popularity and prizing character as well as ability.*
Everyone associated with the Dolphins knows where they are headed and what values drive the journey.

■ KEN BLANCHARD

The problem with most leaders today is they don't stand for anything. Leadership implies movement toward something, and convictions provide that direction. If you don't stand for something, you'll fall for anything.

■ DON SHULA

SHULA

Someone has said that a river without banks is a puddle. When I apply that saying to human interactions, it reminds me of the job of a coach. Like those river-banks, a good coach provides the direction and con-centration for performers' energies, helping channel all their efforts toward a single desired outcome. Without that critical influence, the best achievements of the most talented performers can lack the momentum and drive that make a group of individuals into champions. In my work with the Miami Dolphins over the years, one single vision of perfection has motivated all of my coaching—that's winning every football game. Without exception, every coaching strategy I've adopted has been aimed at that one target. A broad target that's easy to achieve leads to the "puddle" of mediocrity. Keeping that specific focus before the team and con-centrating the efforts within narrowly defined limits are my tasks as the coach of this football team.

I believe that if you don't seek perfection, you can never reach excellence. Maybe it was because I regarded an unbeaten NFL season as a possibility that the feat became a reality. In 1972 the Miami Dolphins won every game, including the Super Bowl. That was the thrill of a lifetime. You may ask, "How can you do any better than that? How can you be better than perfec-tion?" Well, you can't. But it certainly has set a standard that no one will forget and one toward which I want my teams to always strive.

Someone watching a football team consistently pull off brilliant plays might wonder if that kind of suc-cess is not simply a matter of knowing more about the game, being more creative, having better players or a better playbook. Without downplaying the importance of those factors, I'd say that, in the long run, winning coaching has more to do with the coach's own beliefs. If you're going to be a good coach, you may have to set aside temporarily the fascination with game science and look first at what's true for you.

What are your beliefs? This is such an important, first-priority question that I would say your long-run success depends on your answer. Why do I say that this examination of your own belief system is so critical? Because beliefs are what make things happen. Beliefs come true. Inadequate beliefs are setups for inadequate performance. And it's the coach's—the leader's—beliefs that are the most important; they become self-fulfilling.

The realization of a dream like the Dolphins' 1972 unbeaten season is invariably the result of a strong set of operating beliefs and principles that are continually in evidence throughout the formation, training, and day-to-day practice of a team. I always carry with me a set of core beliefs, values, and convictions that support my vision of perfection. These beliefs drive my entire philosophy of coaching. They set the context and the boundaries within which our players and coaches can operate. They also keep me honest and heading in the right direction. My coaching beliefs, in a nutshell, are these:

- Keep winning and losing in perspective
- Lead by example
- Go for respect over popularity
- Value character as well as ability
- Work hard but enjoy what you do

These beliefs are at the heart of everything I do with my coaches and players. Holding to them in actual practice is the basis of my being a winning coach. You won't be a successful leader if you don't have a clear idea of what you believe, where you're headed, and what you're willing to go to the mat for.

BLANCHARD

The Scripture says, "Without vision, the people perish" (Proverbs 29:18). The reason leaders today must begin with a strong vision, and a set of positive beliefs that support it, is that without them, the people they're coaching will not only lose, they'll be lost. Lacking something to uplift their hearts when difficulties arise, their minds will not be equal to the challenge.

I once asked Max DePree, retired chairman of the board of Herman Miller and author of *Leadership as an Art,* what he thought the leader's role was in terms of vision. He said, "You have to act like a third-grade teacher. You have to repeat the vision over and over again until people get it right! Right! Right!" Coach Shula thinks his job is to constantly communicate his vision of perfection to his team so there is no doubt about the game plan. But winning to Don Shula does not mean "no holds barred." His core set of beliefs and convictions sets the boundaries.

A clear vision and a set of operating values is really just a picture of what things would look like if everything was running as planned and the vision was being fulfilled. World-class athletes often visualize themselves breaking a world record, pitching a perfect game, or making a 99-yard punt return. They know that power comes from having a clear mental picture of their best performance potential.

Developing a clear vision of perfection is almost like producing a movie in your mind. I recently had a chance to work with the top management and the heads of dealerships for Freightliner, a leading manufacturer of large trucks. Jim Hibe, the president, spearheaded the development of a new service vision for their dealerships—one that would permit them to go way beyond their competition. In preparation for their key annual conference, they produced a thirty-minute video that illustrated two hypothetical dealerships. The first, called Great Scott Trucking, typified the present mode of operating for many of the dealerships: limited hours (eight-to-five on Monday to Friday and nine-to-twelve on Saturday); uncommitted employees; few, if any, extras (like donuts and coffee for truckers waiting for their vehicles); and so forth. When you entered the dealership, everything seemed to be organized for the convenience of the employees, not the customers. For example, the manager comes in about 11:45 on Saturday. Seeing a long line in the parts department, he says, "Make sure you shut her down at twelve. The line will make for a good Monday."

The other dealership was called Daley Freightliner and was a customer-driven operation with twenty-four-hour service—seven days a week, committed and trained employees willing to go the extra mile, and all kinds of services for the truckers. They had a lounge with LA-Z-Boy recliners and a huge TV showing first-run movies. There was a quiet, dark room with bunk beds in case the truckers wanted to sleep. Employees drove repaired trucks to the front rather than making the drivers retrieve them from the back lot.

Many of the dealerships were closer to Great Scott Trucking than they were to Daley Freightliner, so when the conference opened with the video, it made some people squirm. But it beautifully pictured the new service vision for all to see and experience. I followed the video

with a talk entitled "Raving Fans," all about having customers who want to brag about you. After that, dealers
who were closest to the Daley Freightliner image shared
their success stories. To me that program was an excellent
way to communicate a new vision of perfection.

People are more likely to follow something they can
clearly see. All great companies and teams have a vision-
ary leader at the top who is always pointing to the kind
of organization they're going to be. That vision cannot
easily come from the bottom of an organization. It begins
at the top and is continually communicated from there.
People are inspired by vision. Once they understand the
vision, they consciously and unconsciously begin to move
toward it and even inspire others.

A consultant friend of mine, Barbara Glanz, was doing a customer service session for a large retail grocery company in the Midwest. Speaking to a large crowd of front-line service people—cashiers, baggers, stockers, butchers, bakers, and others—Barbara told them, "Each of you should put your own signature on your job. What could you do that is uniquely you, that tells your customers they are important?" She always leaves her phone number with audiences and tells them to call her to ask a question or to tell about a success that relates to her topic.

Three weeks after her talk, Barbara got a call from a nineteen-year-old grocery bagger named Johnny. The caller, a Down's syndrome youngster, told Barbara, "The night after I heard you speak to us, my parents and I talked about what I could do special for my customers. I've collected good quotations over the years, and we decided I would give them to the people I serve at the store." He went on to tell her that he typed his list of quotes on the family computer, made 150 copies of each, and cut them out and folded them. The next day, he chose one of his quotes, and when he finished bagging a customer's groceries, he'd say, "I'm putting my quote for the day in your bag. I hope it makes your day brighter."

The day Johnny called Barbara, the store manager was making his rounds. When he got to the front of the store, he saw that all the customers were in Johnny's aisle. Johnny said, "When he tried to usher some of the people into other lines, no one would leave. They all wanted to get my quote for the day." Barbara followed up the story by calling the store manager. He reported, "One of the customers told me, 'I used to shop here once a week; now I stop by here every day.' Since the kid's success, everybody on my staff is trying to do special things for customers! For example, the butcher likes Snoopy, and now when people pick up their orders, the packages are sealed with Snoopy stickers. When flowers are damaged, the folks in our flower shop are cutting the broken stems off and making corsages to pin on customers shopping in our store. Everybody who works here has caught the spirit that Johnny started!"

What a difference one person can make in bringing a vision alive! Johnny caught the vision and helped change the service delivery from the bottom up. (And Johnny would probably not have come up with his idea if top management hadn't brought in someone like Barbara Glanz to stress the importance of customer service.) <u>*People need to understand how their work fits with and contributes to the overall goals of the organization. A vision highlights the organization's purpose so that all members are clear about how they contribute.*</u>

It's early on a weekday; most people in Miami haven't had breakfast yet. The sanctuary is cool, dark, quiet. The first rays of the sun are coming through the stained-glass windows, painting the stone floors with shards of color. The silence is broken only by an occasional rustle of movement or a quiet cough from the handful of parishioners who file past the altar receiving communion. As the last of the supplicants turns away, the priest glances toward a rear pew, where a lone figure is bent in prayer. He smiles and thinks, The Dolphins must be back in town.

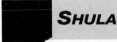

SHULA

My mother and father were both strong-willed, intensely moral people. My mother was raised a Roman Catholic, and my father converted when he married her. A great many of the ideas and thoughts I have, as far as my relationship with God is concerned, stem from those early years and the lessons I learned around the house about honoring God and doing things the right way. For example, we never missed Mass. From second grade on, I went to a Catholic school, including college, and even today I try to attend Mass every day. When we're at home, I attend a small service every morning at 6:30 A.M., conducted by Father Geiser at St. Thomas University. I've known Father Geiser ever since I arrived here in 1970. Attending Mass and looking to God for guidance aren't just habits for me. They matter deeply to me when I'm out in my world of shrill whistles and clashing bodies. And when game day comes, they're ways for me to keep my perspective. It makes a real difference to me when I start off each day by giving thanks and asking for help from God.

Now, please don't get me wrong. I'm no priest, and I'm not saying you should believe the same way I do. But belief in something bigger than you is important. People close to me will tell you I'm not a real pleasant person after losing a football game, but I'd be a lot worse if I didn't realize that something far bigger than football exists. There's something good about kneeling down, asking for help, and listening for answers. My religious beliefs are very personal and private, so I'll conclude with this: If your highest authority is your boss or your organization or, worse, yourself or your last victory, you *won't* be a very effective coach.

Journalist Peggy Stanton included Don Shula among nine men she profiled in her book The Daniel Dilemma: The Moral Man in the Public Arena. *The reason Stanton chose Shula as an example of a moral man is best summed up by his son David, who was finishing up high school when she interviewed him. Today he is the coach of the Cincinnati Bengals.* "You know, those times when we lost the Super Bowl or we lost players that were real valuable—things that really hurt my father and, as a consequence, our family—I could see his devotion to God by the fact that he didn't lose faith, that he didn't give up, he didn't quit. And the reason that he didn't was because he had confidence that someone was watching over him." *To former Shula assistant Bill Arnsparger, recently retired from San Diego and considered one of the greatest defensive coaches in the NFL, Shula has been successful because* "he knows how to separate what's important from what's not important. Don is great because of the decisions he has made. And the decisions he has made have been based on his religion. His faith has made him the tremendous person he is."

During the 1994–95 season, there was always a full house at the Dolphins' pre-game chapel and Mass. In fact, it became an established ritual at the end of each game, win or lose, for regular attendees at these services to invite opposing players of similar faith to gather in a prayer circle in the middle of the field.

BLANCHARD

Norman Vincent Peale always believed that faith leads to positive thinking and patience. When things aren't going right, patience is an energized belief that things will eventually go your way. As a result, you don't give up and start to cheat or lose control or begin to take uncalled-for risks to get the results you want right now. While Don Shula does not consider himself a patient man, his faith gives him a big-picture perspective on things that does not let adversity consume him or let his ego take over. He has winning and losing in perspective.

Elizabeth Kubler-Ross, author of *On Death and Dying* and one of the founders of the hospice movement, said in a recent interview, "The highest ideal we can reach is the original state in which we were created as children of God, with all the love, compassion, and creativity we used to have before we thought, 'We can do it without God.'" This reminds me of some people I meet who occupy leadership positions in industry and act as if winning in business and having God at the center of one's life are incompatible. That view can definitely get in the way of leaders who are trying to "reinvent" themselves.

Acting in traditional ways, leaders today are less and less able to find their way alone through the maze of problems they face. Doing business is becoming much like playing a game, where opponents are multiplied, risks are increased, and the number of factors that could spell success or failure are proliferating. To play this game (especially to win it), leaders must learn to rely on their intuition—that calm, quiet sense from inside that tells you resoundingly what is so, despite outward circumstances that would seem to be contrary. At the same time, leaders must be relentless in their attention to detail, watching for evidences that spell opportunity. This paradoxical equilibrium, between trusting in your own way as you approach danger and calmly discerning the outward signals for action, is actually very close to a quality that has traditionally been called "faith." That's where your partnership with God begins.

It's a wonder to me that practical business people avoid looking in the direction of inner or spiritual guidance for solving their problems. (I addressed this issue in my little book published last Christmas entitled *We Are the Beloved*.) Somehow, organized religion has not connected the idea of God with the nitty-gritty problems people face every day. If faith in God does not help people solve baffling personnel problems that come up in their organizations, or if it serves no purpose in working through the painful issues of downsizing or cutting costs or reengineering, then what good is it? I believe that genuine faith is eminently practical, and that a vast resource for inner knowing stands ready to assist today's leader who will try it.

Good religion is like good football; it isn't talk, it's action. People aren't interested in your religious badge or your theory. They are looking for leaders whose faith works for them on a day-to-day basis.

Success is not forever,
and failure isn't fatal.
■ DON SHULA'S FAVORITE SAYING

SHULA

I don't know where I heard it, but that saying on the previous page has guided my thinking for a long time. It reminds me to keep a long-range perspective on things, to hold the big picture and go for the long run. I don't want short-term ups and downs to be a part of my football game. You just can't afford to let yourself become over-confident through victory or consumed by failure. It tends to divert attention from the business at hand—preparing for the next game. Monday morning after each game, the coaches and I review the game films with the team and extract any possible learnings from the film. After that, whether we've won or lost, we don't mention that game the rest of the week. I want everybody's energy focused on preparing for the next game. Even in the 17–0 season, I didn't let the team dwell on their successes.

As coach, your own mental attitude toward winning and losing is key. If you win, you can't afford to transmit a feeling of arrogance or over-confidence to the team. And if you lose, you cannot afford to engage in blame and negative release. Coaches who experience burnout, even successful ones, do so because they become ground down by negative situations. Magic Johnson, in ending his short coaching career with the L.A. Lakers, admitted he

In recent years, Don has gotten a lot of assistance from two players who help keep winning and losing in perspective. If we've lost a game, and the team gets on the plane in really low spirits, two deeply spiritual players, Keith Jackson and Irving Fryar, go around helping people get up off the ground and come back to prepare for the next game. They also never get too excited when we win. If the players are sky-high after a victory, these guys also help calm things down so we're in mental shape for the next game.

■ MARY ANNE SHULA

couldn't handle defeat. My son David, the youngest coach in the NFL, has had three losing seasons at Cincinnati. No matter how low or discouraged he gets, I tell him he can't let his coaches and players sense that. They look to him for leadership, and he has to stay positive. I'm proud of the way David has done that (even when we beat the Bengals last fall). I was also glad I didn't have to remind my youngest son, Mike, who's a tight-end coach for the Chicago Bears, not to bask too long in victory when they beat us last fall.

BLANCHARD

When *The One Minute Manager* was published in 1982, it began a success spiral that included three years on the *New York Times* best-seller list, and millions of copies sold. For the first time in my life, I was experiencing being part of a huge success. My coauthor, Spencer Johnson, and I became celebrities in the business world. It seemed I had two choices. The first one was to take all the credit and to assume that we were better writers and more insightful thinkers than others and that the book's success was a reward for our talent. The second choice was to follow the path of wonderment. Why had this happened to us, and what could I learn from it? By taking the second path, I began to observe the impact that success and failure have on people.

Most people would say that success is not a problem. They don't realize that success can be just as devastating, if not more so, to some people as failure is. There is an abundance of stories about sports figures, entertainers, and business leaders who went quickly to the top, only to crash and burn. I've also had my share of failures and defeats. After I'd done everything right and achieved my doctoral degree, I was turned down for every job to which I applied. Add to that the fact that I was married, had a baby boy, and had another child on the way. While my college buddies were well on their way to building careers, I couldn't even get a job. I learned then that there are also two responses you can make to failure. You can use that failure to define yourself. Or you can approach it with that same sense of wonder. If I hadn't taken the path of wonderment, I wouldn't be where I am today as a teacher and writer, for I had earlier put all of my expectations toward being a dean of students.

It sounds trite to say it, but one of the marks of real success in life is to believe that there's a reason for everything. We can't control every event, but we can control our response to it. Life is unpredictable. Good and bad fortune that we hadn't planned on will occur. What makes a winner is that when something happens, that person's belief system brings forth attitudes that can take good events and make them better; likewise, it transforms bad events into opportunities to learn. Do you think this has any application in the business world? Hundreds of thousands of businesses are started each year. Within six months, fifty percent of them are dead. Within three years, less than twenty percent will

Coach Shula would always stop by the table I was eating at and thank me for coming. Only one time did I ever get up from my table and talk to him outside the dining room. I noticed he was pacing back and forth. The Dolphins had lost two games in a row and I sensed he was upset. I said, "Coach, there's nothing that a good win can't correct." "Oh no, Tommy," he said, "that's not on my mind. My son David's wife is in the hospital right now, about to give birth." Everybody says Don Shula's mind is fixed on one thing: winning football games. But it was then I saw the human side of Don Shula.

■ TOMMY WATSON,
DOLPHINS HOME-GAME PASTOR, 1972–86

still be alive. If every one of the owners of the businesses that failed defined themselves wholly by that failure, we'd have a lot of people in trouble. Dean Smith, the great North Carolina basketball coach, said it well: "If you make every game a life-and-death proposition . . . you'll be dead a lot." When you feel that failure isn't fatal, you've got the capacity to rebound. This is a lesson that parents have to teach their kids, Little League coaches have to teach their players, and business coaches have to teach their work teams.

I got to witness firsthand Don Shula's capacity to rebound from a setback, in December 1994 when the Dolphins were blown off the field in the second half of a disappointing 42–31 Sunday-night loss to the Buffalo Bills. The Dolphins were 8–4 at the time, and a win over their archrival would insure them a play-off berth and eliminate the perennial Super Bowl contenders. The Dolphins were leading 17–7 at half-time, and then the roof caved in. I was part of a group that waited in the Shula sky box for Don to appear after the game. When he did, he looked completely drained and exhausted. A friend tried to give him encouragement by saying, "Don't worry, Don, you'll get them next time. I know we'll make the play-offs."

Don was quick to intervene. "What I don't need right now is a pep talk."

Shula needed the space to feel the loss deeply so he could then focus his, the coaches', and the team's energy on the next opponent, Kansas City.

When I saw Don on Monday night before his weekly TV show, he was a different person. His mind was already on Kansas City. While he reviewed the Buffalo game on his show, you could see the hurt was over. As we ate dinner and watched the Raiders beat the Chargers, Don Shula had already left the loss behind and was preparing for the next battle. And I'm sure his team was, too, especially the way they blew Kansas City out of the water, 45–21, the following Monday night. After the game, in typical Shula fashion, Don told the press, "We've clinched it. Now we're looking toward these next two games and the best possible situation we can have in the play-offs."

Great coaches are not consumed by their own importance. When they win, they're happy—particularly if the team performed well. When they lose, they're not happy—but they are able to put that behind them. Don Shula is not a great coach just because he's learned how to win, but because he's learned how to handle the inevitable losses that are part of any game. He has managed to keep his ego out of the way. ("Ego," by the way, has been defined as *Edging God Out.*)

People who are ego-driven are dominated by fear and the need to be right. They're afraid to fail because they think their worth as human beings depends on how others see them. They have to keep winning to prove they're okay. To ego-driven people, success is measured only by the number of wins, sales, conquests, or acquisitions they achieve. Great coaches want to win, but they don't fall apart when they lose. When I was working with Norman Vincent Peale on *The Power of Ethical Management,* we were discussing humility, and Norman said to me, "People with humility don't think less of themselves . . . they just think about themselves less." He could have been talking about Don Shula.

It takes a big person to do something like that—admit a mistake and then go to such lengths to right the wrong. One of the most destructive traits a leader can have today is arrogance — acting like you've got it together all the time.

> *Don Shula lost his temper on national television during a heated game with the Los Angeles Rams. Unhappy with the referee's call, Shula voiced his displeasure in language that did not make him proud, especially when an open microphone was carrying his whacks at the Second Commandment ("Do not take the Lord's name in vain") into millions of American homes. He was flooded with letters from people all over the country telling him how he'd let them down. Everyone who included a return address received an apology from Shula expressing his regret without excuses. "Thank you for taking time to write," ran a typical response. "Please accept my apologies for the remarks. I value your respect and will do my best to earn it again."*
>
> ■ PEGGY STANTON,
> *THE DANIEL DILEMMA:*
> *THE MORAL MAN IN THE PUBLIC ARENA*

Confession?

On the other hand, one of the most endearing qualities I think anyone can have is to be in touch with his or her vulnerability. Most football fans are familiar with Shula's jutting jaw and determined scowl as he strides up and down the sidelines, but probably few know the soft, gentle, and vulnerable side of Don Shula. It's that side of the man that keeps his ego under control.

The greatest tribute to Don Shula involved the one tribute his players would not offer Sunday. Respect for the NFL's winningest coach was leaving the Gatorade cooler on the ground. Members of the Dolphins were going to dump the liquid on their leader during the final moments of Shula's 325th career victory, a 19–14 victory over the Philadelphia Eagles. But at the last second, they changed their minds. He had just led them to a second-half comeback with their third-string quarterback. He had just convinced them, once again, to embrace the improbable. They didn't want him looking like a drowned rat. They wanted him looking like a king.

"A classy man," guard Keith Sims said. "We looked at the Gatorade and said, 'You know, we need to do a classy thing.'" And so he was lifted by three linemen and carried across the Veterans Stadium field, his left arm thrust to the sky, his eyes moist, surrounded by dozens of his players straining to touch him. In passing George Halas for the most career coaching victories in NFL history, Shula traveled in style.

■ BILL PLASCHKE, LOS ANGELES TIMES

SHULA

Lots of leaders want to be popular, but I've never cared about that. I want to be respected. Respect is different from popularity. You can't make it happen or demand it from people, although some leaders try that. The only way you can get respect is to earn it. How? Not by talking. People have to see you doing things, time after time, that make sense to them in a larger way; they have to recognize that your actions are motivated not by your ego but by your desire to have them be the best. They don't even have to like what you do in order to respect

I've gotten to the point where I can talk to anyone about what I do. I know my business, and I've gotten where I am because of Don Shula. Now, the process of getting there by working closely with someone like Shula is not necessarily for everyone. It's not always an easy road. It's tough when you stand up in your meeting and start to put something on the board, and there in the front row is Don Shula. He knows football and he knows it well, so you'd better have done your homework. He's always questioning you: "Why? Why? Why?" That makes you question yourself constantly. Because of this, over the years now I've developed such a habit that I'm really prepared. I respect him and I think he respects me.

■ MIKE WESTHOFF,
MIAMI DOLPHINS SPECIAL TEAMS COACH

Mike Westhoff coaches twenty-four hours a day. I couldn't ask for more dedication.

■ DON SHULA

and follow it. The fact that you, as a coach, are asking performers to go beyond themselves, to push their limits, will automatically mean that you'll often be doing unpopular things. If what you're after is being liked, that's going to dictate how hard you'll push; you won't want to offend anybody or get them mad at you. As soon as that happens, there goes your effectiveness; and in the end, there goes their respect.

PURPOSE, PREPARATION

The relationship I want to establish with my football team is one of mutual respect. I want my players to respect me for giving them everything that I have to prepare them to play the best that they can play. My respect for them has to come from knowing that they are willing to give me all that they have to prepare themselves to be ready to play. To get that kind of commitment from people, you can't be worrying about whether they like you or not. The same things that make you successful as a coach make you successful as a father or a husband. I hope people can respect me for the way I run my personal life, as well as for the way I coach the Miami Dolphins.

As long as you have credibility, you have leadership. To me, credibility is your people believing that what you say is something they can hang their hat on— something they can immediately believe and accept. The minute your credibility is questioned in any way, it affects your leadership capacity. When I'm up in front of our team giving information, I want attention and respect. To gain these, I know I must first have trust. It must start with me. I have to be completely honest with my players. If I see a player in the back elbowing his neighbor and whispering to him, I question whether that person believes what I am saying. I immediately stop and confront this situation to find out what is happening. If I am wrong, I want my people to be honest with me, too.

One of the ways you earn respect is to admit it when you've made mistakes. As coach you have to make tough decisions, and this means you can blow it. If you ever make a mistake or don't make the right call, and you don't acknowledge that it was your mistake, that'll eat away at your credibility. For example, in the Jets game last November, with three minutes to go, we were fourth and five in our own territory. Marino wanted to go for it. He was afraid we wouldn't get the ball back. But I figured we had three time-outs left, plus the two-minute-warning time-out. I made the decision to kick. What happened? Jim Arnold kicked the ball off the side of his foot, and it went about thirty yards. (It bounced in a guy's hands, and he fumbled it momentarily. If we'd recovered the ball, my decision would have looked like a great one.) Now the Jets had the ball in good field position, and it looked like they could move it down the field and clinch the game with a field goal or touchdown. But our defense rose to the occasion. We got the ball back, and Marino led us down the field. We scored in the last twelve seconds to win.

Of course, it could have gone the other way, and Marino and the offense wouldn't have had the ball back. If that had happened, and I'd tried to blame somebody else later in the locker room, I'd have lost the respect of the team. When the heat's on and it's your decision, you have to make it. The players know it's your call, and they will respect it.

> *A while back, I tried to give Dan Marino a what-if scenario. I said, "We've scored on the last play of the game. This puts us one point behind. We can kick the extra point to tie the game and force an overtime, or we can go for the two-point conversion, and win or lose. If you lose, everyone says, 'Why didn't you go for the tie?' If you go for the tie but lose the coin-toss in the overtime (we lost ten out of the first twelve tosses in 1994) and don't get a good kick, the game can be over quickly with your opponent's field goal. When this happens, everybody says, 'But we could have won it with a two-yard play!' What's your call, Dan?" He just smiled and said, "Coach, this is why you get paid so much."*
>
> ■ DON SHULA

BLANCHARD

The moment you accept leadership responsibility, whether it's in business, education, government, or the family, the spotlight is turned your way when tough decisions are to be made. How you make these decisions, and whether or not you stand by them will impact your respect and credibility. Sometimes doing the right thing takes on larger meaing—as when you have people's jobs in your hands. If you've been trying to be buddy-buddy with your people, these tough decisions are complicated even more. Emotional attachment has nothing to do with a person's performance

Detachment is part of Coach Shula's style. Charlie Morgan, Don's longtime friend and lawyer, told me some comments he'd heard from Bob Griese and Nick Buoniconti, mainstays of the unbeaten 1972 team. They agreed, "Since we worked for Don we've become better friends with him. When we were players on his team, he was always more detached." Some coaches are described as "players' coaches"; they want the team to love them. Don doesn't care if they like him. That is not his job. His concern is that players be their best. Shula and his coaches will work hard with a player who wants to stretch himself. But if his performance is continually going south, after a while the inevitable "career-planning" talk comes.

> *Shula had to have a "career-planning" talk with kicker Jim Arnold after twelve games in the 1994 season. Arnold had led the NFC and tied for third in the NFL in 1993–94 in gross punting average. The Dolphins had picked him up as an unrestricted free agent from Detroit in April 1994. Shula had high hopes for him. But Arnold was never able to regain his winning form with Miami. Shula released him after the Jets game in November. "I hated to do it; Jim was well liked," he said. "But he just couldn't get the job done for us. Maybe he was trying too hard. But I had to find someone who could rebuild the confidence in our kicking game. John Kidd, a journeyman kicker who'd performed well for San Diego, was available, so we handed him the ball. He made a fine contribution during our play-off drive."*

I see emotional attachment as a problem not only in business, but in schools with teachers, and at home with parents. They often want to be liked. As a result, they may back off from decisions that would push people to be their best. Few of us enjoy making the kind of intervention in which people might get mad at us. And yet, when you think back, the people who were most influential in your life were probably the ones who got into your face when you needed it.

I remember an English teacher named Miss Symmes. All the other English teachers I had had would pat me on the back and give me a B because they liked me and wanted me to like them. Not Miss Symmes. The first essay I wrote for her she returned with an F and told me I was better than that. Since I was already a student leader, I thought I could get by with my gift for gab, but she insisted that I needed to learn to write, too. And she wouldn't back off. She pushed me and pushed me until, on the last paper I turned in to her, she was proud to give me an A. I was proud too. I'll never forget her. I bet you have a "Miss Symmes" in your life.

The bigger issue, though, is: Are you willing to be a "Miss Symmes" to someone else? Are you willing to push your players—whether it's a group of middle managers or a Cub Scout pack—beyond their comfort zone so that they can experience excellence? Being a great coach means sacrificing popularity and being liked, for doing the right thing so that you are respected. In the long run, you'll be remembered as the best coach they ever had.

I don't know any other way to lead
but by example.

■ DON SHULA

SHULA

A lot of leaders want to tell people what to do, but they don't provide the example. "Do as I say, not as I do," doesn't cut it. Of course, I'm not about to show players how to run or pass or block or tackle by doing these things myself. My example is in things like my high standards of performance, my attention to detail, and—above all—how hard I work. In these respects, I never ask my players to do more than I am willing to do. My own preparation for every game has to be exemplary. I am dedicated to success and will do whatever it takes to achieve it. I am generally the last one off the practice field.

I once heard something that pretty much sums up my attitude toward work: To be successful, all you have to do is work half-days; you can work the first twelve hours or the second twelve. During our seven-month season, the coaches really don't have any days off. We work seven days a week. In training camp we move in with the players, and it's almost twenty-four hours a day thinking about football. Our coaches may not take the bumps, the hits, the injuries, but the players know that the toll on us is high.

During the 1994–95 season, I had what I thought was a calcium spur on my heel. It became so painful to move around on the practice field every day that I began to wear something like a ski boot at practice to reduce some of the pain. I didn't want to take the time to correct the problem until after the season. I can't ask my players to play hurt if I wimp out when I'm hurting a little bit. Finally I had no choice. One day in early December, when I was heading off the field after a practice, I felt something pop. It turned out I'd ruptured my Achilles tendon—the same injury that had sidelined Dan Marino for the previous season. (How's that for empathy with

DEVOTION
SACRIFICE
CONSISTENCY
EXAMPLE

the players?) The day I had the operation was the first regular-season practice I had missed in my twenty-five years with the Dolphins.

> *Mary Anne Shula reported, "Don was at the hospital early on Friday morning to begin the preparation for an operation that would repair his tendon. After the operation, he was taken to recovery and then to his hospital room, where he was scheduled to stay overnight. By 2:30 in the afternoon, he'd had enough of the hospital. He asked me for his crutches, and we were on our way home shortly afterward. By 5:30 the next morning, he was up and wanting to attend Mass and then go to practice. I could only get him to relax for a short while. By 10:00 A.M. he was on the practice field in a golf cart. And that was the way he coached on Monday night against the Kansas City Chiefs."*
>
> *With his foot elevated, Shula was driven up and down the sidelines by an aide. After the Chiefs had scored on long drives the first two times they had the ball, the TV cameras zoomed in on Shula directing his driver to where the defensive team sat after they came off the field. He was upset, and he didn't want to leave any doubt about that in anyone's mind. One of the commentators watching this laughed and said, "I think some of those defensive players are lucky that Shula can't get out of that golf cart. . . . If things don't get better, he might drive that cart right onto the field." After Don's outburst, the defense rose to the occasion and helped the Dolphins win this important game and a play-off spot.*

ZEAL, DEDICATION

BLANCHARD

One of the critical leadership issues in our country today is lack of respect and credibility. With all the downsizing, restructuring, and other massive changes going on, the typical employee sees little pain occurring at the top. The huge CEO salaries and perks are particularly annoying to people who are out of a job or whose job is threatened. Sure, top managers get fired once in a while, but the general public sees them waltzing away with fabulous treasure chests.

It may sound as if I'm against downsizing. Not at all. As I mentioned earlier, in today's business climate, nothing is predictable. Change is constant, and that is why it's especially important that top managers or leaders work to maintain their credibility with those they lead. What this says to leaders in every kind of organization is, "Don't ask your people to do what you're unwilling to do." When you ask your kids to clean up their room, and your workroom looks like it was visited by a cyclone—or you insist they be frugal, while you're spending money like it's going out of style—you strain your credibility and lose respect. I see managers getting upset with employees who are late for work, when they themselves take long lunch hours and then are late for meetings, inconveniencing those who are waiting for them. Whether you, as a leader, like it or not, everyone is watching you. Show me a manager who comes in late for work and leaves early, and I'll show you a workforce that mirrors these practices.

One thing that distinguishes successful people from unsuccessful people is that they are willing to go the extra mile—to do what others are not willing to do. Describing Shula's energy and dedication to getting the job done right, longtime friend and former Dolphin assistant coach Monte Clark said, "I think the church he goes to is called Our Lady of Perpetual Motion."

The first week before the opening preseason game, Shula insists that all his players bunk together at the training camp. If the players were required to stay overnight at camp, guess who else was required? I had dinner one evening at that time with the Shulas and with Don's daughter, Donna, and her husband, Steve Cohen. After the meal, Don kissed Mary Anne good-bye and dutifully headed off to camp.

What I've said so far about credibility may sound a little like knuckle rapping or something your mother always told you. Let me try to give it a little bit different spin. One time I was taking Dorothy Jongeward, who cowrote the book *Born to Win,* to the airport after she'd made a great presentation to our staff. I said, "Dorothy, you did such a great job relating Transactional Analysis to the workplace. Nobody could have done it better." She smiled and said, "Ken, lots of people could have done it. But nobody else could have done Dorothy Jongeward. T.A. is the way I choose to share myself."

What would happen if you looked at your job as a manager, teacher, or parent as an opportunity to share yourself? Usually we're so busy with our tasks, we forget that above all else, what our people get from us is *us*—our values, our attitudes, our perceptions. In the long run, it's not our skills or our know-how or our long experience that makes the biggest impact—*we* are the main message! How do you share yourself through your work?

Although I realize that I'm not going to win in the NFL without some extraordinarily skilled players, character has always been just as important to me—and in some cases, more important.

■ DON SHULA

SHULA

I've always felt that you win with good people. To me character is just as important as ability. Character has to do with how people are put together. It's the correlation between what they believe and how they act. Are they dependable? Will they be there when you need them? Once in a while I've hired a player for his ability over his character; and every time, the team has paid for it. If the guy turns out to be a bad apple, then I have to replace him before he influences the rest of the barrel.

Coach Shula is very meticulous. He covers all the bases. He asks probing questions of his coaches. He wants you to know everything about the players for whom you're responsible—how much they weigh, what they're thinking. Some of it may look like baby-sitting, but he wants you totally involved. We are the key people to make recommendations to him about who stays and who goes. He wants us to be as candid as we can be, without being belligerent or negative. Say what you have to say, and then it's up to him to make the final decision. He wants good athletes and good people.

■ JOE GREENE

All the players respect Joe Greene. I depend a lot on Joe's judgment. He's a no-nonsense guy. When he says something, it's meaningful.

■ DON SHULA

At the end of each day during our training camp, I get together with all of our coaches and talk about the practice sessions and the players. I ask each of the coaches to get to know the players well and to find out what makes them tick. I want to know how each player will react in different situations, what his capacity to learn and retain is, how he handles injuries, and what his work and study habits are. The more our coaches can know about a player, the better prepared they are to determine whether that player will fit into our Dolphin system and have good chemistry with the team. A few times, I've tolerated behavior that didn't fit my standards because of a player's unique contribution, but only until I could find somebody better. Generally I would rather pass up someone whose character and personality doesn't match the Dolphins' character profile.

My belief that you win with good people has held up. Through the years, I've had a number of people who, on the surface, didn't possess great ability but who exhibited outstanding character and tremendous motivation. The 1972 perfect season team had numerous examples, like "Mr. Dependable," Howard Twilley, star wide receiver. When you looked at Howard, he wasn't big enough, he wasn't fast enough; but he had the biggest heart and the greatest pair of hands in the world. I would put Nick Buoniconti in the same category. In fact, I call him a classic overachiever. Technically, Nick wasn't big enough, fast enough, or strong enough to play linebacker, but with his great determination, enthusiasm, and love for football, he was one of the best who ever played the game. He was able to adapt and adjust to what was happening on the field—and he made few, if any, mental errors. Offensive lineman Norm Evans and undersized nose tackle Manny Fernandez were like that, too—always there when you needed them. So were our quarterbacks Bob Griese and Earl Morrall. These are the kind of people with whom you want to be associated.

In recent years, I've had some fine players whom I could count on for character leadership. First to mind is fullback Keith Byars, who joined us in 1993 from Philadelphia. That first year, he had a great season and was chosen our MVP. He's a first-rate guy. He never misses a practice, and he gives you 150 percent. So does wide receiver Irving Fryar—a real positive man we got from New England—and also tackle Rich Webb.

Dan Marino is a natural leader. You have to admire the way he came back from the Achilles tendon injury that ended his 1993 season. When he arrived in camp last summer, he was hungry to play. He wanted the big game—the Super Bowl—and so did I. I need guys like these who are ready to take leadership roles where and when it counts.

When the players first come back to camp to begin preseason training, we do a 300-yard shuttle run to see what kind of shape they're in. It's back and forth in these lanes against the clock and the running backs have to make it in fifty-four seconds. Every-

Intangibles are the hardest things to read. How do you test for spirit? There is no test for it. The best predictor is past behavior. When we go to a school, we talk to the trainer and the conditioning coach. We even talk to the equipment man—he usually knows what kind of guy this kid is because he sees him when he's most relaxed. Even when you have them here for a year, though, some of them surprise you in a positive or a negative way. A few years ago, one of our leading pass receivers was making a million-dollar salary; then he went off and got himself in trouble with drugs and eventually self-destructed. We finally had to let him go. Tom Heckert, the player personnel director, has to tell guys they are through. That's a thankless job but a necessary one. We just can't afford to have people on the team who don't fit our character profile.

■ Tom Braatz,
Miami Dolphins
Director of College Scouting

one is sucking air. They're glad when it's over. At training camp in 1994 I looked up and saw Keith Byars running one more shuttle. Afterward he said, "That one was for the Super Bowl!" How can you ask for better leadership by example than that? It really hurt us when Keith got injured in the middle of the year and was lost for the season. Sometimes that kind of spirit and character leadership becomes contagious.

Some of you might remember a tradition with the 1972 Super Bowl team: to sprint to the other end of the field at the end of the third quarter, when everyone is usually dragging. I have a hunch that not every Dolphin felt like running, but when a guy sees his captain leading the way, the enthusiasm rubs off.

It hurts when someone with real potential doesn't have the desire. I had one kid who I thought was going to contribute, but we couldn't get him to come back to practice. He's gone. Ten years from now he's going to be asking whether he had the stuff to make it in the pros. He had a chance, but you can't help a guy if he won't show up.

I like to give every opportunity for a player to prove himself. A while back, we had a guy here who was big and strong enough to bench-press a house—but he never had heart. The guy never could cut it. We spent a fortune, blew a big bonus on him. I finally let him go. After two years, he was still missing his assignment. He couldn't line up, couldn't remember plays. On one simulated play, he missed his man, and Marino would have been sacked. This guy said, "Let's do it over." But you don't do it over. In life, you don't get two chances.

BLANCHARD

When my wife, Margie, and I started our company, we decided that we would only hire people that we liked. Our rule was that if we saw somebody coming in the front door and didn't feel a chemical change in our bodies—a change that would mean we were really glad to see them—then we wouldn't hire them. That was easy when we were running a small mom-and-pop operation, but we still think it's important. Our three main operating values are (a) *ethical*, doing the right thing; (b) *relationships*, building an environment of trust and respect; and

(c) *success,* accomplishing our organizational goals. Recently we had to make the tough decision to end a relationship with our top producing trainer, because he kept on violating our two top values, ethics and relationships. Things like that are never fun, but if you don't have people who have the inner character that you want, you're constantly distracted.

Someone once asked Mary Kay Ash, the founder of Mary Kay Cosmetics, how she was able to get all of her salespeople to be so nice. She said that what she did was hire nice people and then create an organization in which they could be just as good as they were. I gave a speech recently at the Ritz-Carlton at Laguna Niguel, California. This hotel had just been chosen the number one resort hotel in the United States. Some of the participants in my session asked me how they got people at that hotel to go out of their way so often for their guests. During the break I approached two Ritz-Carlton employees and asked them, "Do you all go out of your way for your customers because you're just good people, or are you trained to do that?"

"Both," they said. "We hire good people, but we put them through an extensive training program that includes a two-day orientation and a twenty-one-day supervised work experience. At the end of this time, the new employee sits down with us to evaluate their future with the company."

If you want to win with good people, you can't leave it to chance. You have to hire, train, and supervise people to operate according to the values for which you stand.

The master in the art of living makes little distinction between his work and his play, his labor and his leisure, his mind and his body, his information and his recreation, his love and his religion. He hardly knows which is which. He simply pursues his vision of excellence at whatever he does, leaving others to decide whether he is working or playing. To him he's always doing both.

■ JAMES MICHENER

SHULA

People ask me all the time, "Don, what motivates you? What keeps you doing the same thing for over thirty years?" My answer is always the same: When the stadium's full, the crowd is yelling, and the referee raises his hand to signal the start of the game, I can feel the adrenaline rushing through my body. I wouldn't want to be anywhere else in the world. I think it's fabulous that I get paid for doing what I love to do.

A front office job is not my cup of tea. I love football and I love to coach. The competition was what attracted me to the game—this and the mental aspect. You have to be physical, you have to have great athletic ability, and you have to know what you are doing. And you have to have desire. I want to win them all, but if something happens and I lose a football game, I want to get as much out of the experience as I can and then use it the next time we compete. I'm always looking forward to the next game.

To me the enjoyment of coaching is not a perk; it's an essential ingredient of winning. This is why it's on my list of convictions. Sometimes they'll put the camera on the coach during a football or basketball game, to show his joy or his outrage at some event. People want to see that passion in the leader; it's inspiring to think that all this commitment and energy is behind your team's performance. You can't fake your love of the game; it's there or it's not. If you find you like coaching, give it all you've got. If not, let someone else do it.

Ken and I were watching the Florida-Alabama game last December. At half-time the duo of Terry Bowden, head coach at Auburn, and his father Bobby Bowden, from Florida State, were talking about who should be the national champion. On satellite they got coach

Joe Paterno of Penn State involved and asked him who he thought should be the top team—his own Nittany Lions or Alabama, who was undefeated at the time, or Big Eight champion Nebraska. Joe just didn't even want to deal with it. He said he was personally thrilled for himself

> *When it comes to a head coaching job, if it happens, it happens. The important thing is that I enjoy what I'm doing. When I stop enjoying it, I'll move on to something else.*
>
> ■ JOE GREENE,
> DOLPHINS DEFENSIVE LINE COACH

and his team that they were going to the Rose Bowl. He didn't want to take away any of the joy of this experience by getting involved in a foolish argument about the national championship. I couldn't agree more with Paterno. The press wants to suck us into these kinds of comparisons and crystal-gazing conversations. I want to enjoy the thrill of coaching one game at a time.

 BLANCHARD

In most people's eyes, there's a big difference between work and play. Work is thought of as something you have to do, while play is something you choose to do. To me the distinction is more an idea than a reality, since both require physical and mental energy. Confucius said, "Choose work you love, and you will never have to work a day in your life." The greatest job is when you're confused about the difference between work and play. The best managers in the world are those who absolutely love what they're doing. Don Shula is a great coach because there isn't anything he'd rather be doing than coaching his team toward a victory. One thing that will help you make sure your work is also your play is to develop a personal mission statement.

The crux of a mission statement is identifying what it is you enjoy so much that you lose track of time when you're doing it. I've noticed that I'm happiest and at my best when I'm teaching or writing. (For example, I just noticed that it's 4:00 A.M. as I'm writing this.) I also want my life to make a difference in others' lives. So my mission statement reads: *To be a loving teacher and example of simple truths that help myself and others to awaken the presence of God in our lives.*

I say "awaken the presence of God" because I acknowledge that there is a higher power in my life. Perhaps we've taken a risk with some readers by mentioning God in this book, but I think all of us can get ourselves into trouble if we believe there's nothing more powerful and knowledgeable and loving than ourselves. In the fall last year, Margie and I were leading a personal excellence seminar at Yosemite Park. One of the participants objected to my references to a higher power. Later in the weekend, we took people up to Glacier Point, a breathtaking summit 3,000 feet above the valley floor, to work on their mission statements. I noticed my unbelieving friend standing at the edge, looking thoughtfully at the gorgeous spectacle. I walked over to him, and the two of us stood there for a few moments, taking it in. Then I said, "It's a beautiful accident, isn't it?" We both laughed.

I think the greatest addiction in the world today is the human ego. As I said earlier, EGO stands for *E*dging *G*od *O*ut and putting yourself in the middle. One of the joys of working with Coach Shula is that he has effectively integrated his love of football, his desire to make a difference in the world, and his devotion to a higher authority. You can achieve the same balance in your life by developing a mission statement and keeping it foremost in the decisions you make regarding your career.

SECRET #2

OVERLEARNING

The essence of coaching is the <u>attention to details and the</u> <u>monitoring of results</u>—these are what help leaders realize visions and accomplish goals. This is what Shula calls over-learning. The overpreparation that Shula insists on is based on his overlearning system: limiting the number of goals and things players work on, cutting down on players' practice errors, making players master assignments so that players can operate on autopilot, and operating on a philosophy of continuous improvement. He believes in achieving practice perfection.

■ KEN BLANCHARD

Entering the hospital, the man takes an elevator to the second floor and asks for directions at the nurses' station. His face is solemn as he walks down the hallway toward the designated room. He enters and moves toward the bandaged figure on the bed. The patient sees him, smiles wanly, raises an arm from which tubes dangle.

"Thanks for coming, Coach."

"How you doing?"

"Oh, okay." The mournful look in the sunken eyes tells a different story.

There is a long pause. Finally the visitor leans in, his jaw jutting close to the face of the patient.

"Listen, Mike. I need you in training camp in July—on the field, ready to go. We're going all the way this year."

Later Mike Westhoff, recovered from bone cancer and still the special teams coach for the Dolphins, would say of Shula, "I thought he would tuck me in, but he didn't. He treated me the way I could be, not the way I was."

SHULA

My ultimate goal for all our players, given the limits of each one's talents, is performance at the highest level possible. I figure that if our coaching staff can get maximum performance from each player, the team will give us everything it has to give. I also know that it's not just a matter of mathematics—instead, when the whole team is cooking, and all the pistons are firing together in synch, synergy kicks in, making the team much more than just the sum of its parts. Because I know that perfection only happens when the mechanics are automatic, I insist on overlearning.

Overlearning means that the players are so prepared for a game that they have the skill and confidence needed to make the big play. More than anything else, overlearning—constant practice, constant attention to getting the details right every time—produces hunger to be in the middle of the action. When players have absolutely no doubt about what they're supposed to do or how to do it, they thrive on pressure. If the heat's on, they want it coming their way. If the player is a halfback, he wants the ball. If he's an end, he wants the pass thrown to him. If he's a lineman, he wants to make the important block or tackle. I don't want my defensive halfback praying that the ball is thrown to the other side of the field. I want him to want the ball coming his way.

That kind of desire to be in the middle of the action was a characteristic of the 1972 championship team. I decided to alternate Mercury Morris and Jim Kiick at halfback. I felt that with some teams, Morris would be a better asset, and with other teams, Kiick should be the man. Whoever didn't play as much on a particular Sunday was always in my office on Monday, complaining about it. They wanted the big play; they wanted to be there. Neither of them wanted to be on the sidelines when there was action on the field.

Our staff works hard with our players to instill pride in practice performance, giving everything they can in daily practice—the part the crowd and the reporters never see. The concept of practice perfection is difficult for some players to understand. Many times when they go out on the practice field, they're tired or they're beat-up from the previous week's game. There I am, asking them to pick up the tempo, be on top of their play mentally and physically, be sharp in their practice execution. Sometimes these players would rather take the easy way. Like kids, they complain that "none of the other teams practice this hard" or "other teams don't wear pads this often in their practices." Right! Those are usually the teams who have disappointing seasons.

It may be a cliché but it's true: you play at the level of your practice. The best way is to practice hard all the time. I am convinced that the coaches and players both must know that the overlearning system works. That means they must understand all four components of it:

1. Limit the number of goals
2. Make people master their assignments
3. Reduce players' practice errors
4. Strive for continuous improvement

One thing I hate is a blown play. You know, the center snaps the ball, the quarterback takes the snap and pivots to his left to make an inside hand-off . . . and no one is there! It's the Keystone Cops in football shoes. If we're lucky, we make it back to the line of scrimmage and only lose the down. Usually we get thrown for a loss. And do you know what caused this blown play in the first place? Someone was thinking too hard about what he was supposed to be doing. The play was called in the huddle, and the running back wasn't sure if he was to go slightly right or straight ahead. He's still wondering when the play begins, when he should just react. He should have known the playbook so well that when the play was called, he would have gone on autopilot and gained the seven yards that the play was designed to produce.

BLANCHARD

Shula's overlearning principle is based on high expectations of people. People generally respond well to leaders, managers, coaches, and parents who have high expectations and genuine confidence in them. J. Sterling Livingston, in his classic *Harvard Business Review* article "Pygmalion in Management," refers to Eliza Doolittle's words to Colonel Pickering from the musical *My Fair Lady*: "You see, really and truly, apart from the things anyone can pick up (the dressing and the proper way of speaking and so on), the difference between a lady and a flower girl is not how she behaves but how she's treated. I shall always be a flower girl to Professor Higgins, because he always treats me as a flower girl and always will; but I know I can be a lady to you, because you always treat me as a lady and always will."

Livingston found that some managers always treat their people in a way that leads to superior performance, but that most managers, like Professor Higgins, unintentionally treat people in a way that leads to a level of performance that is lower than they are capable of achieving. The way managers treat people is powerfully influenced by what they expect of people. If a manager's expectations are high, productivity is likely to be excellent. If expectations are low, productivity is likely to be poor. It is as though there were a natural law that caused a person's performance to rise or fall to meet his or her manager's expectations. My wife, Margie, has often said that one of the reasons she didn't get into trouble when she was a young person was that she knew her parents expected the best of her and knew she would be a good role model for her younger sisters. She never wanted to let her parents down.

If you have someone working for you whom you don't think much of, I think it's your ethical responsibility to get them transferred to another department or team. Because no matter how hard you try, you're likely to treat them as if they aren't any good. And they'll prove you right every time! I ask people all the time, "Given the amount of time you spend at work, would you rather spend that time being magnificent or ordinary?" What do you think they say? They shout out, "Magnificent!" And yet, are most of the people in organizations performing magnificently? Of course not. And a key reason is the self-fulfilling prophecy that starts in leaders', managers', coaches', and parents' heads, with the belief that most people are lazy, unreliable, and irresponsible. This belief plays out in how they treat people, and ultimately in how these people perform.

Is there any wonder that Don Shula has been successful in getting the most out of people? His overlearning system demands high performance from his players. His expectations of his coaches—and even of the referees—keep them constantly "performing up." He is always demanding of himself and others. There is no clearer example of this Shula characteristic than his treatment of special teams coach Mike Westhoff when Mike was stricken with cancer.

Former referee Art Holst contends that what separates great coaches like Shula, Landry, and Lombardi from everybody else is that they have tougher expectations of their players than their players have of themselves. "Shula can look at talent and see what they could do. Whether the players think they can or not, he can sense how great players can be. He thinks coaching is getting your players to the place where they realize that they can be that good and then they actually do it. Shula has the same attitude about officials."

Coach doesn't tolerate weakness or lack of concentration in himself. He works hard and he expects his people to do the same. He was very demanding, even when I was sick with cancer. I showed up at training camp with crutches, a giant brace, and no hair. Often I would leave the office and go outside and throw up because the chemotherapy was affecting every part of my body. One day we were in a meeting, and Don and I got into a disagreement about a kicker (I turned out to be right: the kicker wasn't very good). Not only did Don not baby me, he was blasting me up and down, back and forth. I knew I was right, but he made sure I'd done my homework.

That day I got so involved with what I was doing that I didn't get sick, and that night I ate a full meal. At the time I wasn't ready to say, "Thanks," but when I look back today I realize that it was because Don didn't treat me as if I were an outcast that I worked so hard to prove to myself that I was right—and then felt perfectly normal. When we were coming out to play the Steelers in the last game of the year, the brace I'd been wearing all season broke. I took it off and never put it on again. Coach never said a word. I coached the whole season with a cane. I'll always be grateful to him for helping me develop the mental toughness you need to function no matter how you're feeling—to function like a normal person with normal responsibilities. Don Shula never looked at me as if I were handicapped. He sees what you can be, not what you are.

■ MIKE WESTHOFF, MIAMI DOLPHINS SPECIAL TEAMS COACH, WAS GIVEN SPECIAL RECOGNITION FROM THE DOLPHIN PLAYERS FOR HIS COURAGE DURING THE 1989 SEASON. AS A RESULT, HE RECEIVED THE NFL'S ED BLOCK COURAGE AWARD.

Jim Tunney, retired thirty-year veteran NFL official, agrees. "Shula expects so much of himself and his players that he also has very high expectations of officials. He expects you to be in the right position to make a call, so he wants you to be hustling all the time. Also, he thinks you should not make a call if you're out of position. Shula knows what position you need to be in to make every call.

Other coaches don't have a clue, except maybe one or two. If you make a call that hurts the Dolphins and you're not in the right position, you are certainly going to know it. Shula will be right on top of you. He is considered hard on officials, but I feel there are two reasons for this. First, Don is on the rules committee and probably knows the rules better than any other coach in the business. Second, he practices with officials present at his preseason practices. He works hard with his players to get them to know what the rules are and live by them. Therefore, when a whistle is blown to call a penalty on a Miami player, Shula's assumption is that it has to be a mistake of the official because his players certainly wouldn't risk his wrath by making this kind of mistake." Need I say more about the power of Don Shula's lofty expectations? Do people perform better when they are around him? His record speaks for itself.

> *Shula never stops expecting the best of people. We will be ahead in games by three touchdowns, with only two minutes left, and he'll still be going 150 miles an hour. You want to say, "Hey, Coach, it's okay, we won the game. Relax a little."*
>
> ■ DAN MARINO,
> ALL-STAR DOLPHIN QUARTERBACK

I think goal setting is overrated.

■ DON SHULA

SHULA

Setting goals is important, but I suspect that most organizations overemphasize this process and don't pay enough attention to what needs to be done to accomplish goals. I know that this is true in the NFL. Most teams start their training camps at the same time and begin their preseason activities with a team meeting. At this meeting, the head coach usually gets up in front of the squad and the coaches and outlines a list of goals and objectives that he wants them to accomplish that year. Most coaches say the same thing: they want to make the play-offs and, in a perfect world, win the Super Bowl. To me, what's often more important than these goals is the follow-up—the attention to detail, demand for practice perfection, and all the things that separate the teams that win from the teams that don't. These details also separate the successful head coaches from those who get fired. Here's where the importance of a game plan comes in. Let me describe what we do.

As quickly as possible after a game, my coaches and I analyze the game film so we can give the players feedback the next day. For years I used to give the players the day after the game off (usually Monday). The last few years I've brought them in on Mondays to: (a) get a look at them physically, in terms of what kinds of damage the game might have caused, (b) have them run a bit, (c) show them the tape so everyone can see what we did well and what we could improve.

Tuesday is the players' rest day, but a long working day for the coaches. This is when we do our planning and develop our game plan for the next opponent. After analyzing all the different things our opponents have been doing lately on defense, we pick out what we think has the highest probability of success from all the choices we have offensively against their defensive formations. We might even invent some new plays. This is all written down and distributed to our offense as their game plan. The same procedure is repeated to produce a defensive game plan. But this time we are choosing what we think has the highest success probability against our opponent's passing, running, and specialty game. A weekly defensive or offensive game plan can run over thirty pages. (I laugh when I think that when I first started coaching in Baltimore, the specialty team game plan was on two sides of a sheet of paper. Now that, too, can run over twenty pages.)

As information technology gets better, managers get finer, more detailed information to use for analysis. This could immobilize some people. To Don it is exciting. Technology, particularly video, has made a major change in coaching football. When he first began coaching, if during practice Don observed something he wanted to remember, he had to shout to someone on the sidelines with a clipboard. Now everything is on film for player, coach, and opponent to view. Do you look at the increased information available to you for decision making with the almost childish delight that Don Shula experiences? Listening to him describe his game plan made me understand why he likes the analogy of the head coach being like a general preparing for battle.

■ KEN BLANCHARD

When the players come in Wednesday, we're ready to give them our game plan and focus our energy toward the next game. Every day from now on has its own life. Wednesday is our offense day; we go over the offensive game plan page by page with the players. We don't want to leave any doubt in their minds about how we intend to play on offense in this next game. Some of this explanation is done in front of the entire team, but most is done by the assistant coaches who have responsibility for a particular area of our offense. When everyone knows what we have in mind, we start putting it together on the field. Our defense simulates the opposing team's formations throughout this practice.

On Wednesday night we prepare for Thursday and focus on our defensive strategy. Again, we go over the defensive plan page by page and then put it to work on the practice field. Our offense simulates the opposing team's offensive patterns throughout this practice.

After practicing these combinations on Thursday, that night we prepare for Friday, when the emphasis is on the green zone—the area inside the twenty yard line. (Some people call this area the red zone; we call it the green zone because this is where teams cash in on field position.) On Friday we work on both our offense and defense in this zone, and our kicking game. Saturday is rehearsal day; it is low key, and we walk through our plays. No one is wearing pads or attempting to work up a sweat. This is like the dress rehearsal before a show. Show time is the next day. Throughout the week we're continually adding and subtracting things from the plan and polishing it, until by game time we have our short list—the stuff we really like. These plans are put in protective wrapping, and we carry them with us on the sidelines.

It's in the implementation of our game plan that goals get accomplished. The game plan provides the mechanism for focusing our efforts toward our vision of perfection: winning every football game. This is where the real coaching takes place.

BLANCHARD

How's that for a close-up of the incredible amount of meticulous detail that a successful coach is willing to put himself and his team through to win games? I seldom

see this level of preparation in other organizational settings. I see people showing up to sales calls unprepared,
knowing little about their customers. I see people chair-
ing meetings who've given little thought to their strategy
to accomplish the agenda. I hear parents wondering what
they can do to help their kids perform better in school. It
seems the American way of managing is for managers to
set goals, file them (in folders or in their minds), revisit
them at the end of a performance period only, and then
wonder why things didn't go the way they wanted.

Goal setting is important. All good performance
starts with clear goals. Goals point people in the right
direction. Goals begin the accomplishment process. But
it's the coaching—observing and monitoring, day in and
day out—that makes the critical difference. Can coaching and attentive follow-up make a difference in the business world? You'd better believe it. Let me give you an
example.

A longtime friend of mine, Bob Small, is the Don
Shula of the hospitality industry. We grew up together in
New Rochelle, New York. Just as Shula learned the game
of football from the bottom up as a player, Bob started
washing dishes at a local restaurant when we were in high
school. When he decided to go into the hospitality business, he wanted to learn every facet of it. Among his early
jobs he worked as kitchen manager at The Four Seasons
in New York City and as executive assistant manager at
the five-star Arizona Biltmore. When he was ready to take
over his first hotel, he sought out Willard Marriott Sr., the
founder of the Marriott hotel chain. Marriott took an
immediate shine to Small and decided to find out how
good he was by having him open the first Marriott hotel
in Europe, in Amsterdam. When Small completed that
project successfully and brought the hotel to a high

European rating, he and Marriott conceived of and built the Rancho Las Palmas Marriott in Palm Springs. It took Small less than five years to bring the five-star designation to that resort. After a short tenure as a regional vice-president, Small left Marriott to lead the turnaround of the Americana Hotel in Fort Worth, Texas, owned by the Bass Brothers. That having been accomplished, Small opened all the new hotels in Disney World and then took over the leadership of the Fairmont Hotels. Recently the Fairmont Hotel in San Francisco was reinstated as a Triple-A diamond property.

Like Shula, Small didn't become a success by accident. His game plan mentality is similar to Shula's when he takes over an operation. Every position is analyzed. Every customer contact point is put under close scrutiny. Every department and position, in essence, develops its own game plan around Small's vision of perfection: to be five-star, to be the best, to be the standard by which the industry is judged.

My son, Scott, during his hotel administration study at Cornell University, took nine months off to do an internship under Small when Bob was beginning his turnaround of the Americana Hotel. Scott talks about the energy that was generated when Small called a meeting of all employees to announce the change in the name of the hotel to the Worthington, which better described Small's vision for the hotel. On each person's chair was a Pledge to Excellence form which the employee was asked to sign. At the end of the meeting, every employee went forward to hand in his or her signed pledge and to receive a five-star lapel button to symbolize the destination. (At Disney, Small gave all the resort cast members a D.R.E.A.M. pin to symbolize that *Disney Resort Experiences Are Magic.*)

Small, like Shula, doesn't miss practice. When he took over the Americana, he'd heard that a number of employees had been going across the street and drinking with guests, so during the meeting he made it very clear to employees that their job was not to fraternize with customers but to serve them. Despite this, the day after the meeting, some people had gone drinking again with guests. Bob crossed the street and announced that they should report to his office as soon as possible so they could pick up their final checks.

Scott did a stint on the front desk during his internship. When his trial period ended and Bob, in reviewing Scott's performance, found Scott was regarded as too laid back and lackadaisical, Small got right in Scott's face, and they agreed he would repeat the front desk trial period. These incidents made a lasting impression on Scott. To this day, when he's talking to me about Bob, he calls him Mr. Small.

Shula and Small are the best at what they do. Do you want to be the best? If you do, remember: goal setting only starts good behavior. It's the follow-up—the attention to detail and the monitoring and the coaching—that makes it happen. As Small says, "The destination is marvelous, but the real joy is the journey."

I want our players to be so familiar with their assignments that when the game starts, they don't have to worry about what they're supposed to be doing. They can simply turn themselves loose physically to do whatever it takes to win the game.

■ DON SHULA

SHULA

If our players are worrying about their assignments, they have a tendency to hold back. I want them out there turning it loose. They should be so familiar with their assignments that when the game starts, they're operating on autopilot, the way you do when you drive a car: you're not thinking about what your hands and feet are supposed to be doing, you're just doing it. When players are completely undistracted, they can let go and do what's needed, at the time it's needed. This is why the playbook everybody gets at training camp is so important. Everything they need to know about their position is in there. It's a lot to learn for a rookie or some- body we've picked up in a trade or as a free agent. The first week, we're patient. But the second week, we're starting to expect them to know their basic moves. I learned the playbook concept from Paul Brown, my first coach as a professional player.

You can tell when a team is up for peak play, even before a game. All their energy is going toward playing their best, working together. None of their attention is being drained away by worry about mechanical trifles— what-do-I-do-whens. When these interferences are eliminated, players are more likely to get into the "zone" where peak performance is possible. This is what I mean by being on autopilot.

When a person's on autopilot, the mental picture he carries matches the potential moves his body will make as the play comes off. He is not thinking of these things; he is simply doing what he has seen and felt a thousand times as he has run through this play in practice. His body will move on its own like a machinery of reflexes. Then his mind can be thinking ahead, anticipating the opportunity to make something important happen.

The most obvious place where spectators can see this happening is with the quarterback. When Marino sets back into the pocket, he doesn't have to think about what he wants to do, so he's able to sense danger and move out of its way, often just in the nick of time as he releases a pass downfield. For Marino to be successful, he has to have receivers who are doing the same thing. They must know their patterns forward and backward so they can concentrate on getting to the ball, even in heavy traffic.

BLANCHARD

The "autopilot" concept is important not only in sports but in other areas, such as public speaking. When I'm really prepared for a speech, I find I'm able to improvise and be creative in ways that significantly enhance my presentation. Why? Because I'm not worried about what I'm going to say. When you get to that level of preparation, you don't need a coach in the traditional sense—someone to tell you what, how, when, and where to do something. You're able to coach yourself in that performance area. Being able to function on autopilot frees you up to achieve higher levels of performance.

Tim Gallway, author of *The Inner Game of Golf,* says that achievement is the result of skill minus interference. By "interference" he means the self-talk that tends to clutter up the mind of the average golfer during performance: "Keep the head down! Watch the left arm! Follow through!" Focusing on mechanics will immobilize the golfer, and it's the same in business. Consequently, you have to be just as tenacious in orienting your people to their assignments as Don Shula is.

In sessions in which I have hundreds of people from different companies in my audience, I often ask how many have a well-organized orientation program. Less than ten percent of the hands go up. Is there any wonder why these companies don't get the performance or behavior they want? No one can suit up at Disney, even part-time, unless he or she goes through a supervised two-day Disney Traditions program. The first morning of the program, they show movie clips of Walt Disney and his dream of a Disney empire. They run fun games and contests to help the new employees get a sense of the history of Disney. The next three half-days, people learn about the company's operating values and how these translate into their behavior on the job.

The values statements of many companies sound like God, mother, and country; nobody knows which value is most important, much less what it means for his or her job. Disney doesn't leave this to chance. When you ask people what they remember most about going to a Disney park, it's usually the cleanliness of the park and the friendliness of the employees. The values that drive these customer impressions have been emphasized during employee orientation as well as during the follow-up supervision given during the early days on the job. Maybe you've noticed that when a Disney employee sees a piece of paper on the grounds, he or she will automatically bend over and pick it up. This is no accident. Cleanliness is one of the chief values at Disney, and when supervisor after supervisor models the cleanliness value by helping clean up the grounds, it doesn't take long for new employees to go on autopilot for this part of the job. In fact, when you comment to Disney employees after they've picked up a piece of trash as you've been walking with them, they'll tell you, "I didn't even realize I was doing it. It's just part of being a Disney cast member."

What is the goal of the autopilot concept in business? It's to free people up to do on their own what they've learned reflects the values, goals, and standards of the company—and to be creative the rest of the time. This is exactly what Don Shula is after in his players. He has no need to direct anyone if they are able to direct and monitor themselves. He wants all his players to know their assignments so well that they don't have to think about mechanics, they can "just do it!" He feels the same way about his staff. Ryan Vermil-

Once my wife and I were invited to a Boston Celtics "shoot-around" (or what we would call a practice) the day before a Lakers-Celtics game in Los Angeles. I'll never forget Coach K. C. Jones' comment when I asked him, "How do you coach superstars like Larry Bird, Kevin McHale, and Robert Parrish?"

"I just throw the ball out and once in a while I yell, 'Shoot!'"

That's the ultimate in self-monitoring.

■ KEN BLANCHARD

lion, head trainer for the Dolphins, told me, "Coach Shula puts pressure on his staff from the beginning. When I first came here, he was on top of me for everything. It seemed like he was closely supervising my every move. It was tough at the time. He was constantly testing me; he wanted to see how I responded to pressure and whether he could trust my judgment. Now he knows he can let me alone and I'll get the job done. He coaches you so you do your job and he can count on you."

Football is a game of errors. The team that makes the fewest errors in a game usually wins.

■ PAUL BROWN,
LEGENDARY COACH OF THE CLEVELAND BROWNS,
AND AN IMPORTANT MENTOR TO DON SHULA

SHULA

To me a game doesn't end when the clock finally runs out. It ends on Monday, after we've analyzed every play and learned all we can from it. Once we've established a game plan based on this analysis, our goal each and every week as we prepare to play the next opponent is to cut down on practice errors. If we are able to do this, we increase our chances of playing error-free in the game. We can't expect to play well on Sunday if we had sloppy practices during the week and failed to emphasize execution and perfection. It just doesn't happen. Affirming and redirecting is where we outstrip the competition. I think every mistake should be noticed and corrected on the spot. There's no such thing as a small error or flaw that can be overlooked. If a player makes a mistake, one of our staff will instantly blow a whistle, correct or admonish him, and then make the player go back in and do it right.

Paul Brown's belief that the team that makes the fewest errors wins, certainly applied to the Dolphins' perfect 1972 season. All-star linebacker Nick Buoniconti was proudest of the fact that our defense that year made the fewest errors by far in the league. You could almost count on one hand the number of mental errors they made during that entire 17–0 season. They just didn't make mistakes. They also took pride in being called the "No Name Defense." This name meant they were a team first.

BLANCHARD

Most people think of failure as bad. A friend of mine gave me a new definition for failure. "Failure," he said, "is successfully finding out what you don't want to repeat." In business, we tend to be event oriented. We move from one crisis to another, hardly stopping to see what happened. This leads to denial, so that when there's an error, we almost tend to look away from it rather than toward it—like a golfer hitting a bad drive and not wanting to watch as it heads for the woods. But how can we improve if we don't learn from our mistakes? I know of one company that celebrates mistakes by shooting off a cannon. They're not saying they enjoy making errors; they're announcing that it's time for everyone to learn something they don't want to repeat.

The old rule in business was, "When it's over, it's over." The new rule should be that an event isn't over until after you've learned from it. People in organizations today should develop a fascination with what doesn't work. If, like Coach Shula, you spend part of your time concentrating on eliminating practice errors, you'll also eliminate a good amount of the second-guessing that goes on. Don Shula's method of reducing practice errors echoes a five-step plan for coaching people that I've emphasized over the years:

1. Tell people what you want them to do
2. Show them what good performance looks like
3. Let them do it
4. Observe their performance
5. Praise progress and/or redirect

Managers most often miss the fourth step: *observe.* They give directions, then clear the area. If you don't stay around to watch, you have no data with which to do the last, most important step: *catch them doing things right, or else redirect their efforts.* Recently I was in a McDonald's and observed some wonderful coaching. I ordered a Big Mac and a Diet Coke. The young woman who waited on me said, "How about a piece of apple pie?"

"I thought you'd never ask," I agreed.

As she turned to get my order, I noticed a young man follow her over to the food area. I heard him say, "Good job. That's exactly what we were talking about. Keep it up." Obviously McDonald's was teaching their folks about "up-selling" and its impact on the per-customer check. But I was impressed that here was the manager, right nearby, ready to notice. Affirming and redirecting is where Shula and his staff shine. You can't leave performance to chance. As a coach, if you let errors go unnoticed, you'll ensure that more of them will occur.

> *When I was at the Dolphins training camp, I watched Joe Greene work with Tim Bowens, Miami's number one 1994 draft choice. Tim's a 315-pound defensive tackle from Ole Miss, who played only one year of college ball. He has a lot to learn, but Shula and his staff think he has the potential to be a great player. Joe was close at hand all the time. When they were practicing the blitz on the quarterback, Joe watched Tim like a hawk. Bowens has amazing strength, so it almost takes two offensive linemen to contain him. Joe was trying to emphasize the importance of going in low to maintain a low center of gravity. One time, Bowens went in high. An offensive lineman, who was much smaller than Bowens, brought his arms up and knocked Bowens on his butt. Joe roared with laughter. Then he went over and helped Bowens up. He put his big arm around him and said, "You see what happens when you go in high?" The next time, Bowens did it right; he broke through the line and would have sacked the quarterback in a game. "That's it!" yelled Joe Greene. It's this kind of monitoring that helped Tim Bowens to be named the defensive Rookie of the Year by the Associated Press.*

The Miami Herald's *Dave Barry once labeled this as a nightmare scenario: You're in the express checkout lane, limit ten items. You have eleven items. Running the cash register is Don Shula.*

SHULA

People say I'm intense. I don't know how to behave differently. I believe in what I do. I've got the courage of my convictions. I demand discipline. I don't keep anything inside me. What you see is what you get. Sometimes I'm not very proud of what comes out, but at least it doesn't stay inside. I guess I'm not afraid to let fly because I want to use this energy to build emotional response. Football is a game of guts. I want my players pumped on game day. I don't ever want it said after a game that our opponent's emotions ran higher than ours or that they wanted the game more than we did.

On October 2, 1994, I had the opportunity to play against my son, David, who was coaching the Cincinnati Bengals. This was the first matchup in any sport between father and son coaches. It was a special day and one I'll always remember. I was also happy when it was over and we had won. My wife, Mary Anne, was the only member of my family who was rooting for the Dolphins. My kids all felt that David needed the victory more than I did. In my heart I might have agreed with them, but my responsibility was to the Dolphins. I couldn't let family feelings enter into the game. I want to see David win, and win a lot. I just didn't want to see him win that Sunday.

If I stop getting nervous or anxious before games, that's the day I'm going to hang it up, because in this business, when you start taking things in stride, there's going to be somebody out there who's going to work a little harder and longer. And they're going to beat you because they're a little more anxious.

BLANCHARD

When I work with a top manager, one of the first things I look for is how involved he or she is in the overall workings of the organization. If there's a passion and an intensity, I know the manager cares and wants the organization to be the best. But if the manager seems distracted or not sure about what's going on, I know that in this organization, people's desire for excellence may be lacking. Our company has done a fair amount of work over the years in organizations headed by Marvin Runyon, presently Postmaster General of the United States. Wherever Runyon's gone, he's been passionate about pushing the organization to be more efficient. He was that way at Nissan and at the Tennessee Valley Authority, before he took over the post office. A few years ago, when I finished writing my customer service book *Raving Fans* with Sheldon Bowles, I wanted to rush a copy to Runyon, so I told my secretary, Eleanor Terndrup, to send him a copy the quickest way possible. Not even thinking of the postal service as a means of fast delivery, Eleanor mailed my book to the Postmaster General via Federal Express. According to reports, when Runyon received my package, he not only did not open it, he threw it across his office and out the door!

When I found out what had happened, I called Marvin to apologize. He was on his way to the airport, but his secretary gave me his car phone number. When I got through to him, I said, "Marvin, I owe you a One Minute Apology for sending my new customer service book to you by Federal Express." When he heard that, Runyon began to roar with laughter. "I didn't know it was a book about customer service. Boy, do I have one on you now, Blanchard!" That story has been heard in Runyon's speeches around the country whenever he's talking about customer service.

Intensity is the theme of many Shula stories. I love the one about what happened in the Miami Dolphins locker room a few years ago after a game against the New York Jets. The Dolphins had won, but Shula was not pleased with their play. He had a few choice words he wanted to share with the team. (Mel Philipps, who coaches the defensive backs, told me, "Don is sometimes tougher on the team when they win than when they lose. He knows that the team is stronger when we've won and that when we lose, they're already feeling bad enough.") As he entered the locker room to speak to the players, Shula saw someone he didn't recognize. "Who the hell is that?" he shouted. Someone answered, "He's a writer." "Get him out of here!" Shula commanded. With that, James Michener left the Dolphins locker room.

Intensity matters as never before in business these days. The important thing is not just being intense but focusing that intensity on the things that matter. The other day, the hotel elevator I was riding on stopped at a floor and one of the hotel managers stepped on. He was evidently in a hurry, poring over a big bunch of reports as he hurried them upstairs to somebody. "Got some pretty important stuff there?" I asked. "Nah," he said. "Urgent, not important." This matter of distinguishing what's urgent from what's important is one place where people need a lot of coaching. Charlie Morgan says, "Shula works not only hard but smart. He's a master delegator. During a game, you'll see all his coaches running around with headphones on, and he's standing there with his arms folded, concentrating."

While Shula gets upset, he's also able to let it pass. He doesn't dwell on things. Referee Art Holst said, "Once a game is over, as far as Shula is concerned, it's over. I've never seen a quote from him in the paper saying that the officials lost the game." Shula doesn't like excuses. If a close call by a referee goes against the team and perhaps decided the game, he concludes that the team should have been better prepared to win by a higher margin.

SECRET #3

AUDIBLE-READY

Audible-Ready *is Shula's term for adaptability. Don Shula doesn't believe in holding to a game plan that isn't working. The key to being adaptable is to be well prepared in the first place. "Audibles" are well thought out and choreographed ahead of time. Shula is always asking, "What if . . . ?" so that when a change occurs, neither he nor his players are caught flat-footed. A fixed game plan or published organizational chart can be deadly to organizations today.*

■ KEN BLANCHARD

I don't get consumed by circumstances that are beyond my control. If I worry, it beats everybody else down. I'm always into what's happening next. So Bob Griese has a broken ankle? Okay, let's get Earl Morrall ready and put him in there.

■ DON SHULA

SHULA

Preparation means everything to me. I'm passionate about my players being ready for anything. Now, part of being ready is being able to shift your game plan at will. I see myself as a battlefield commander who has the guts to make the right moves to win. I want to be prepared with a plan —and then to expect the unexpected and be ready to change this plan. I must preserve the right to change—even to change at the last moment—as circumstances demand. Sometimes before games I hear coaches express certainty of winning. They act like the hay is in the barn. But I never feel this way. Right up to the opening moment and throughout the game, I want our coaches and players to be open to changing as necessary to get the job done.

> *When the Dolphins were en route to their perfect season, they had the services of a fine punter named Larry Seiple. Shula told Seiple he was free to run any time from punt formation—as long as he made the first down. In the AFC championship game against Pittsburgh, Shula was surprised when Larry faked a punt on fourth down and ran for 37 yards to set up the Dolphins' first score. As he watched Seiple take off and start to run the ball, Shula started yelling, "No! No! No!" Then when he saw Seiple in the clear, he changed it to "Go! Go! Go!" That was a real audible!*
>
> ■ CHARLIE MORGAN

I want to be doing on the spot what it takes to win the game, not sitting around afterward and learning what I should have done. This is the reason why, during a game, if our quarterback or defensive captain sees the opposing team doing something unexpected, he has to be able to call an "audible." An audible is a verbal command that tells our players to substitute new assignments for the ones they were prepared to perform. Audibles are not last-minute orders the quarterback has dreamed up out of nowhere. They're strategies the players know about and have practiced. I want the team to be "audible-ready"—not only ready to change a play or a formation but to change a game plan if necessary.

Sometimes something will happen beyond your control, like an injury to a key player, and require you to change not just an occasional play but your whole game plan. In 1965 when I was coaching the Baltimore Colts, our all-star quarterback, Johnny Unitas, was out with injuries, and so was our backup quarterback, Gary Cuozzo. Both were great passers, but I had no other quarterbacks on the team, so I used Tom Matte, a halfback, at quarterback in the play-offs. Tom had had some quarterback experience at Ohio State, but back then, under Woody Hayes' offensive philosophy ("three yards and a cloud of dust"), the quarterback was mainly a blocking back. I changed the game plan to take advantage of Matte's running strength, and it worked. Tom didn't know the plays from quarterback, so we ended up writing them on his wristband. We won a crucial game against the L.A. Rams, earning ourselves a play-off shot at the Western Division crown, against Green Bay. One of Matte's famous wristbands resides today in the Football Hall of Fame in Canton, Ohio. I've got the other one in my office.

■ DON SHULA

Sometimes it takes guts and ingenuity to change the plan. Dan Marino's fake grounding of the ball in the last 38 seconds of our second Jets game in 1994 is a perfect example. It looked like improvising, but it was something we started to work into our two-minute drill that year. Bernie Kosar, the quarterback we picked up from Dallas to be our insurance policy for Marino, had experimented with the play at Cleveland and also at Dallas. To pull the play off, the situation has to be just right—a time when the other team would be expecting the quarterback to try to stop the clock by throwing the ball to the ground (that is, legally grounding the ball). When our quarterback is going to ground the ball intentionally, he yells to the team, "Clock! Clock! Clock!" This signals everyone to line up to

> *Shula listens to advice, then makes a decision and moves forward to implement it, without looking back. The coaches who burn themselves out are the ones who are always second-guessing themselves. The players respect a coach who's not wishy-washy. It gives them confidence to have a leader who has no doubt in his mind once a decision is made about which way he wants to go.*
>
> ■ JOE GREENE

protect him while he throws the ball to the ground. This in turn stops the clock so we can get into the huddle and call the next play.

In the game against the Jets, it was the ideal situation: 38 seconds to play, and we still had one time-out left. Bernie's on the headset with Dan and sends in the word. Dan yells, "Clock! Clock! Clock!" and the linemen get ready to block. Dan makes eye contact with Ingram, the receiver on the right side. Dan takes the snap, calmly steps back, looks at the ground, and fires the winning touchdown pass to Ingram as the Jets stand there flat-footed, anticipating the stopping of the clock. It couldn't have worked better.

Even the perfect season of 1972 called for some dramatic adjustments. In week five, Hall-of-Famer Bob Griese suffered a leg injury that ended his regular season play. I turned to Earl Morrall, the veteran quarterback who'd played for me in Baltimore. It was Morrall who led us to eleven straight victories and a spot in the Super Bowl against the Washington Redskins. But at this point, with a healthy Bob Griese now available, I faced a dilemma. Who should start against the Redskins? I'm not one to back away from a tough decision, and I decided to go with Griese. When I told Morrall of my decision, his reply was, "If you need me, I'll be ready." We won of course, but I have to credit Earl Morrall for his fine example of character and class.

Since I arrived in Miami in 1970, it's been reported that our teams are 28–8 in regular season games started by a reserve quarterback. In the record-break-ing game with Philadelphia on November 14, 1993, I faced another no-fun decision. All-star quarterback Dan Marino was out for the season, and his backup, Scott Mitchell, who had led us to five straight victories, went down with a left shoulder injury early in the second half. Doug Pedersen, a man who had never thrown in an NFL game, was the only available quarterback. We quickly changed our game plan, started running the ball, and left the game in the hands of our defense.

"Pretty strange, huh?" Pedersen asked reporters, noting the irony that someone such as he would be a quarterback on this monumental day. "I mean, he's coached Johnny Unitas and Dan. What's a guy like me doing out there today?"

I see no point in sticking with a game plan that's not working. I also don't believe that the sun rises and falls based on my own judgment. I'm continually out there scanning for data that will make my decisions more in-telligent. I make my offensive and de-fensive coordina-tors and assistant coaches respon-sible for their area and for communi-cating with their players. It's their

Mercury Morris commented on an area of adaptability that most people would not consider when talking about Don Shula: "In 1970, two years after Martin Luther King Jr. was killed, Shula brings in Afro Sheen and Afro combs and puts 'em in the locker room, where only Vitalis and Brylcreem had been, if you know what I mean. He was trying to relate. It was a sincere gesture. Shula has had the ability to adjust to the times and to the people who represent those times. Here's a guy who used to have a rule that you couldn't have a beard if you had hair on the top of your head—like, you couldn't have hair 360 degrees. Now he's got Louis Oliver, who wears two earrings just a little smaller than basketball hoops."

■ QUOTE TAKEN FROM SPECIAL SHULA EDITION OF THE *MIAMI HERALD*, NOVEMBER 15, 1993

job to relay any pertinent information that develops during the practice week or during the game. I listen to them, and once I've heard the information, I'm willing to make the decision.

BLANCHARD

Audibles aren't surprises—just new ways of doing what you already know how to do. Business people need to learn to call audibles, because in today's world, nothing stays the same. Peter Vaille, in his book *Managing as a Performing Art,* compares the turbulence felt in the business environment these days to a roaring river; he says we must learn how to live in "perpetual white water." How do you develop top performers to navigate through constantly churning waters? Shula's example provides the answer: prepare them to be "audible-ready." Begin with a map of the river, identifying and anticipating obstacles. Make sure you have the necessary supplies and beware of being burdened with too much weight. Become a "what-if" person like Shula. Shula knows the hand he's holding, but he's always creating possible future scenarios: What if Unitas gets hurt? And Cuozzo too? Or Griese? Or Marino? And, God forbid, Scott Mitchell too? This "what-if" thinking of Shula's works in his favor. While he did adjust well when each of these situations actually occurred, the moment when the need arose was not the first time he'd thought about it. If a scenario he's imagined occurs, the decision to be made at the time doesn't have to be made off-the-cuff. It's when you're caught surprised or flat-footed that you don't have the time to properly evaluate, and you end up making bad decisions. Shula never lets this happen.

Many organizations today have an organizational chart with everyone in a comfortable box. It might look nice on the wall but it locks everyone into a fixed game plan and often into fixed rules. It doesn't give the organization the power to respond quickly to new demands by calling audibles. It's the companies that are constantly adapting that are making striking advances today. An example happened to Tom Cullen, a teaching colleague at the Hotel School at Cornell University. He was having dinner with a family that included a thirteen-year-old son and two younger kids at a fine gourmet hotel restaurant in New York City. When their waiter gave each of the three a children's menu, the older boy was upset. The attentive waiter, reading his nonverbal cues, quickly brought him an adult menu.

The two younger kids ordered macaroni and cheese from the children's menu. When dinner came, they played with the macaroni but didn't eat much. When Tom tasted it, he thought it was something "to die for." It was the best macaroni and cheese he had ever tasted. When the waiter asked the kids if there was something wrong with their meal, they said "It's yucky! It's not Kraft."

The next evening when the family appeared at the restaurant, the waiter from the previous night spotted them and came right over to the kids. "I was hoping you would come back. I got Kraft for you." With that, he went to the kitchen and returned with a box of Kraft Macaroni and Cheese. Can you imagine what a special relationship that waiter must have had with the chef for that kind of adaptability to take place? Is there any wonder why that restaurant is flourishing?

The need for flexibility has led to the current trend of downsizing. Without this de-layering strategy, companies like Wal-Mart, with only four layers of management, would continue to kill bureaucratic competitors with twelve layers. More and more companies are scrambling to get into the position that the Dolphins achieve under Shula's command: the ability to substitute plays and formations at will in order to get the job done in a changing environment. The ability of nimble service corporations to suddenly transfer their energies in order to solve a customer's problem or meet a market's sudden need is the very characteristic Shula calls "audible-ready."

Of all the bureaucratic departments I've had to deal with over the years, the Department of Motor Vehicles (DMV) has to have been the most dreary and demeaning. I used to think the DMV hired only employees who hated people; the employees seemed to take delight in telling customers that they were in the wrong line or had filled out a form incorrectly. I always tried to avoid direct interaction with the DMV; but several years ago, three weeks before I was due to go to Europe, I lost my driver's license. Needing to get the renewal procedure going fast so that my new license could serve as a backup to my passport, I asked Dana Kyle, my executive assistant (who runs my life), to schedule a three-hour block of time at the DMV. I figured that was about the amount of time they needed to beat me up properly.

I headed to the DMV, fully expecting the same old treatment, but to my surprise, I found that a transformation had occurred. A woman employee greeted me as I entered: "Welcome to the Department of Motor Vehicles. Do you speak English or Spanish?" Taken aback, I mumbled, "English." She ushered me to a counter, where I was met by a smiling young man who asked how he could help me. When the procedure was over and I had my new license, the total time—including having my picture taken—had been nine minutes!

"What are you all smoking here?" I asked the woman taking my photo, "This isn't the DMV I used to know and love!"

"Have you met our new boss?" she asked, smiling and pointing to a desk situated smack in the middle of the service area. I walked over to say hello to a pleasant middle-aged man who told me his role was to be a "signal caller and dispenser of resources." As we talked, I saw that he was a man who obviously enjoyed his work, took pride in his organization, and cherished a vision of building a customer service organization. His commitment to doing whatever it takes to get the job done well—the job of serving citizens—was obvious. For instance, he didn't schedule any employee's lunch break between 11:30 and 2:00 P.M. because that's when most people tend to visit the DMV office. He'd also cross-trained the staff, including the secretaries in the back offices, so that anyone could take photos or serve at the front desk. If the number of customers suddenly increased, he could swiftly reorganize the office to meet the demand. This guy knows what it means to be audible-ready. Do you?

SECRET #4

CONSISTENCY

Shula's treatment of individuals is predictable. His focus is always on how they can be their best. His consistency *is legendary. If performance is going well, he's ready to praise, but if the team or a player isn't living up to his high expectations, he's ready to redirect or reprimand. Shula behaves the same way in similar circumstances. It's not the mood he's in but people's performance that dictates his response.*

■ KEN BLANCHARD

The Miami blitz is on. A defensive tackle breaks through the offensive line and nails the quarterback for an eight-yard loss. The opponent will have to kick on fourth down. Shula is the first one to greet the tackle as he comes off the field. "Nice job!"

■

It's third and three. The hand-off is to the running back. He slices through an opening in the line, sidesteps a linebacker, and cuts for the sidelines. It's a footrace, and he wins. Miami touchdown! Wait, there's a flag down at the forty. Oh, no! Holding called on Miami. Forget the touchdown. You wouldn't want to see the look on Coach Shula's face.

SHULA

Consistency is vital in the way you respond to people's performance. I pride myself on the fact that our players can count on our coaching staff to be constantly observing and responding in a consistent manner. If the team ran a play poorly in the preseason and didn't hear a whistle and get redirection, they'd think our staff had gone brain-dead on them. They would also think something was wrong if they ran a play correctly and didn't get some recognition. Good performance should always be treated differently than poor performance.

Your team will soon learn what your standards are and perform accordingly. I not only insist on practice perfection, I'm there to see that it takes place. I don't miss practices. I need to be out there smelling out whatever isn't working. Even the slightest deviation from perfection needs to be noticed and corrected on the spot. Correcting and redirecting performance is strategically important—it's where we outstrip the competition. Some coaches will let little things go. Right there is where the difference is made. To me, it's not a matter of how many times we've done it or how late it is or how tired the players are. We'll do it until we get it right. Then we won't deviate from it in the game. I'd rather throw out a play or formation during practice than find out it can't be done correctly in the ball game. We seldom try anything on game day that we haven't been able to perfect in practice. If I'm asking our players to do something they can't do, I want to know about it *now.*

No matter what the reason, you can't let poor performance go unnoticed—even from a superstar. The same goes for good performance. Never let your mood determine how you respond to a person. Performance is all-important; that's what you need to respond to on a consistent basis.

BLANCHARD

To me people have the wrong idea about consistency. They think it means behaving the same way all the time. I believe that if you praise people and are nice to them when they're performing well and also when they are behaving poorly, that's inconsistent. Consistency is behaving the same way in similar circumstances.

Don Shula is nothing if not consistent. His game plan, his organizing of preseason training, and his preparation for every game are examples of his established patterns. What we're talking about here is a special kind of consistency—responding to people's performance. When you respond to your players in the same way under similar circumstances, you give them a valuable gift, something they have too little of these days, something they'll play hard for. It's the gift of predictability.

In my work with Robert Lorber on *Putting the One Minute Manager to Work*, we contended that four kinds of consequences can follow a person's performance:

1. *A positive consequence.* Something good occurs (from the person's perspective)—for example, a praising, a recognition, a raise, or a bigger opportunity to perform. If a reward or positive consequence is given, the person is apt to repeat the action. People tend to move toward pleasure. Positive consequences motivate future behavior.

2. *Redirection.* Performance is stopped, and the person's efforts are rechanneled to do correctly what they were doing incorrectly. If a person is redirected to do something correctly, he or she is apt to continue doing it

correctly. Redirection can be a powerful way to get people to refocus their behavior.

3. *A negative consequence.* Something bad occurs (from the person's perspective)—for example, a reprimand, a punishment, a demotion, or a removal from an activity. People tend to move away from pain. If an action produces undesirable consequences, the person is apt to avoid it.

4. *No response.* Nothing is said or done following the action. Good actions that receive no recognition at all are apt to be discarded eventually; bad actions will continue unchanged. The only exception is when someone is self-actualizing—that is, they love what they're doing, and will continue to do it well regardless of whether they receive any recognition.

Most people would divide the relative importance of goal setting and managing consequences into 75 percent and 25 percent, respectively. The reality is just the opposite: 25 percent of what impacts performance comes from setting goals, and 75 percent comes from what happens after goals are set. Performance is influenced most by consequences—that is, the response from a coach who is on the scene.

One thing I never want to be accused of is not noticing.

■ DON SHULA

SHULA

Late last season, when I missed practice to have my Achilles tendon repaired, the press made a big deal about it being the first regular season practice I'd missed in my twenty-five years with the Dolphins. I don't know why people make much over my never missing a practice. It's inconceivable to me to be absent when the team is practicing. Coaching to me means being present, on the spot, alert in all my senses to whatever is going on. I don't attend practices for the players; I do it for me. To make the call or decision to change, I have to have nothing between me and what is going on. I want to see what's happening for myself. I also don't wear earphones during games. If I need information from above, I can always get it from my assistant coaches on the sidelines. When I go into a game, I want to be totally available to each and every situation I'm confronted with. I don't want any interferences or secondhand opinions.

I don't see how anyone can be a good coach or manager without being directly involved. I've heard of

> *The coaches are allowed to walk up and down the sidelines between the 35-yard lines only, but Shula sometimes forgets. I've found him all the way down to the 5 yard line. He wants to be lined up nose-to-nose, right on the line of scrimmage, so he can see what's happening. He's amazing. He can see simultaneously what the offense and the defense are doing. He can read the defense, and he knows where the opposing quarterback ought to be throwing; if the quarterback throws to the wrong spot, he knows that. He has incredible knowledge of the game. He can see all twenty-nine people at the same time—twenty-two players and seven officials. He knows what they're all supposed to be doing and when they're supposed to be doing it. It's unbelievable.*
>
> JIM TUNNEY,
> NFL OFFICIAL FOR OVER THIRTY YEARS

guys who delegate so much that they don't need to stick around the office. Personally, I think they're lousy managers. I'm all for delegating, but the buck really stops at my desk. If the Dolphins lose a game, no one blames the special teams coach, the line coach, the backfield coach, or the coach who scouted the opposition last week. They

> *A lot of people think Shula's just a tunnel-vision guy and that all he cares about is what he's calling on third and seven. That's not true. He wants to know everything going on within this organization that he's responsible for— and some things he's not. It's easy to deal with a guy like Shula, who thinks that what you're doing is important.*
>
> STU WEINSTEIN,
> SECURITY AND COMMUNITY RELATIONS,
> MIAMI DOLPHINS

blame me. So even though I give my assistant coaches pretty much of a free hand in developing their special areas of the team, I'm right there every day watching everything. And if I see something I don't like, I make it a point to discuss it with the assistant right then. You can't manage from the press box. You've got to be down on the field with your team. Coaching is an intensely personal business. You can't coach people from a distance, with aloofness. People need to see that you're at least as interested as they are in what's going on.

BLANCHARD

In the typical organization, the most frequent response people get to their performance is no response. We have a name for the kind of manager who only notices employees when they make a mistake. We call this a "leave-alone-zap! manager." You leave the person alone long enough for them to fail, then you move in and zap them. The leave-alone-zap! is the main strategy in what I refer to as "seagull management." Seagull managers fly in, make a lot of noise, dump on everyone, and then fly off somewhere. Let me give an example of why this approach is inappropriate and self-defeating for a coach.

Studies show that among teenagers, there are significantly less incidents of drinking, drug use, indiscriminate sex, and fatal traffic accidents occurring before 12:00 midnight than after that hour. Suppose that the parents of a sixteen-year-old learn about this and say, "We'd better get our son home earlier." They announce to him, in no uncertain terms, that they want him home by 12:00 midnight. The next time he's out with his friends and sees it is 11:30 P.M., he says, "My parents want me in by twelve. I've got to leave." His peers start shaming him: "What are you, man, a momma's boy? Are they going to tuck you in?" He's getting a negative response from his all-important peer group. He's a good kid, though, so he bears the negative response and says, "No, I've gotta go." But when he walks in the door on time at home, where are his parents? They're either gone or asleep. He's lucky if he gets a lick from the dog. This is a typical no-response.

Now let's see how the "leave-alone" results in a "zap!" First, let's look at the score in terms of who has noticed what: so far, the teenager has one negative response (from his peers) and one no-response (from his parents). Which will have the greater effect? Negative noticing will win, going away. It's no contest. Most people will be impacted more by a negative response than by a no-response. This is why it's so important to be there to praise good behavior. In some companies we give managers a set of buttons that read, "I was caught doing something right" and tell them to give a button to an employee when they notice good performance. The recipients appreciate this.

If this is a typical no-response case, what happens when the boy goes out the next night? At 11:30 when he makes his announcement that he needs to be home by midnight, his friends start in on him again. This time he thinks to himself, "Am I crazy? I got home last night on time and nobody noticed. Why should I take this grief from my buddies?" Tonight he arrives home at 1:00 A.M. Where are his parents this time? They're at the door yelling at him, "We told you to be home by twelve! We're sick and tired of your lousy attitude." Seagull management in action. This puts the kid in a lose-lose situation: if he does what his parents want, he gets beat up by his friends; if he does what his friends want, he gets grief from his folks.

This is the kind of bind that people in organizations get caught in all the time. Their managers don't pay attention to what they do until they foul up. If they do what their boss says, their coworkers are upset. If they do what their coworkers want, their boss is upset. The only way to turn this game around is for their managers to start to accentuate the positive and catch them doing something right.

And, of course, accenting the positive works best of all, because a positive noticing usually beats a negative noticing, hands down. Again, it's no contest. It's important to be there to praise the good behavior so that you send some points up against the negative ones that the peers are bestowing. And if you want your children to be home by a certain hour, do whatever it takes to be there to reward their good behavior. If you're asleep, set an alarm. If you're out with friends, announce to them by 11:30, "We told our son to be home by midnight, and we want to be there when he comes home." When the kid walks in, make a big fuss over him, hugging and kissing him and making a big show of celebration. Sound corny? Guess what—it works. My sister and I never stayed out late because the moment we left the house my mother would start baking things for our return. We came home early because it was a good deal! There were all kinds of goodies waiting for us. Old-fashioned? Sure, but our friends loved to come to our house, not only because the food was great but because my mother would play the piano and everyone would sing and dance.

I can't say enough about praising. If people know that their good performance will be noticed and rewarded, it's a tremendous motivator. Positive consequences encourage people to repeat good behavior. And if you're not involved with your people, you won't notice their good work. Like Shula says, you can't manage from the press box.

*The key to developing people
is to catch them doing something right.*

■ KEN BLANCHARD AND SPENCER JOHNSON,
FROM *THE ONE MINUTE MANAGER*

SHULA

Recognizing good performance is an important part of my coaching. I like to recognize our players in front of their peers. My coaches and I will stop and give a player a pat on the back or recognize a great team effort on the spot, but we'll usually repeat the feedback at a team meeting to give our players full recognition. I believe in spreading praisings out so that every contributor receives attention. The actions of the offensive backs, ends, linebackers, and defensive halfbacks are pretty obvious to everyone, but what about those unsung heroes in some of the less visible positions? For example, special teams traditionally go unnoticed by sports fans. As head coach, I can't afford to let this happen.

Years ago I started a meeting pattern to help recognize the less-publicized players. The day after a ball game, our team and coaches review our performance. I will make some opening remarks to the squad, critiquing what happened during the game—good, bad, or otherwise. Then the entire squad views the game films that focus on our special teams. We use this time to create opportunities for players to appreciate each other's efforts. It makes special team players feel they are an important part of the team when a star like Dan Marino says, "Hey, that was a great hit!" After the squad meeting, the team breaks up into groups according to the players' positions. Each group reviews its own game films, and the head coach in each area—together with the players—provides the appropriate recognition, as well as any necessary criticism for that small group.

All this talk about recognition may go against your notion that coaches are effective when they're toughest and most demanding. This is just an impression that's been developed through the national media. Still, although

recognizing good perfor-
mance is important, we
need to place performance
recognition in its strategic
perspective. Good coach-
ing doesn't mean telling
everyone they're doing
great. You want to support
people when they're first
learning, then gradually get
more choosy about when
you give them praise.
When our staff is teaching
something new in pre-
season training camp, we

*One of the key plays in the Dolphin,
wild-card 27-17 victory over Kansas City
was an interception of a Joe Montana pass
late in the game. The interception was
made by J. B. Brown with the Chiefs on
the Miami 5-yard line. It was reported
that when Brown got to the sideline, still
clutching the football, he was told by
fellow defensive back Troy Vincent that he
ought to get the ball painted to celebrate
the occasion. "You just intercepted a
legend," Vincent said.*

give the players a lot of support. Later, when the season
starts, we expect more; therefore we praise less. The goal
is to have players praising themselves and each other for
a job well done. This is when you see all the high-fives on
the sidelines and the celebration in the end zone.

*It became a common occurrence during the 1993–94 season to look over in
the end zone, following a Dolphins score, and see Keith Jackson, Irving Fryar,
Mark Ingram, and Keith Byars (depending on who was in the game) kneeling
down in prayer. After a game against the Jets that featured a last-minute
victory touchdown, the December 5, 1994, issue of* Sports Illustrated
*reported, "In the moments after the play, Marino cavorted at midfield like a
dog in a Frisbee-catching contest. By contrast, Ingram and tight end Keith
Jackson knelt in prayer in the end zone, for the fourth time in the game.
'Thank you, Lord,' said Ingram, the unlikely hero. 'I give you all the glory.
I am only a vessel for you on earth, working for you.'"*

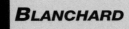

BLANCHARD

People often ask me, "What is the one most significant thing you've learned about managing and motivating others?" I tell them that, without question, it's the concept of "catching people doing something right." Of all four consequences, the positive consequence is the one that will most increase the likelihood that a behavior will be repeated. There are all kinds of positive consequences. Bob Nelson, who is one of my colleagues, being Vice-President of Product Development at Blanchard Training and Development, recently wrote a best-selling book entitled *1001 Ways to Reward Employees.* Nelson spent three years surveying 1500 companies to find out the most effective and innovative ways that managers use to "catch people doing something right." The organizations Bob has written about have learned the power of recognition. A few examples might be helpful.

Tektronix, Inc., a Beaverton, Oregon, manufacturer of oscilloscopes and other electronic equipment, has notecards with the heading "You Done Good Award," on which managers and other employees can write down a personal thank-you and deliver it to another employee. Bell Atlantic's cellular telephone division in Philadelphia names cell sites after top employees. Sherpa Corporation, a software company in San Jose, California, uses an old ugly bowling trophy purchased at a pawnshop as a "pass around" award for spectacular results achieved; the trophy has taken on real significance among the people in the company.

Our experience is that most people tend to take care of others first and serve themselves last. So last year at Christmas at Blanchard Training and Development, in addition to giving profit-sharing checks to employees to celebrate our good year, we gave each employee a 50-dollar bill and an hour and a half to go out and shop during work hours to buy themselves a gift. People were then to come back and share with everybody what they had purchased. People loved it. The laughter and smiles were contagious and memorable as everyone held up and described what they had purchased for themselves. For many, this was the first time they had done something *just* for themselves.

An interesting finding from Bob Nelson's research is that a significant gap exists between what managers believe motivates employees most and what employees say motivates them. Managers often thought that all people wanted were money and promotions. But the highest incentives found, in study after study, had to do with praise and recognition: personal or written thanks by one's manager for good performance, public praise for good performance, morale-building meetings to celebrate successes, and so forth. Also, people felt best if their promotions were based on performance. In the past, most promotions had nothing to do with performance, and more to do with a person's political abilities in moving up within the organization. Today, people want to be recognized for their performance.

P&R (praise and recognition) is an important part of a successful team. If you watch a Dolphins game carefully, you'll see Shula and his staff constantly patting players on the back and praising their good performance. And when something good happens, watch how players reinforce each other's outstanding plays, with hugs and slaps on the helmet. But does this happen routinely in business organizations, where most of the working people in our society play their team games? Hardly. Over fifty percent of the employees surveyed reported that the top incentive—personal thanks from one's manager—was seldom, if ever, being given.

Why don't managers take a few moments to specifically and sincerely thank their people for a job well done? I'm not sure. Perhaps today they're too focused on doing what's urgent to take time for what's important. Maybe they're afraid that to praise employees will lead to requests for salary increases—or maybe they just don't have the skills or the comfort level themselves to adequately praise others. Whatever the reasons, it's becoming increasingly clear that P&R, or cheerleading, is no longer a significant part of managing. And yet, today's employees want to be appreciated and recognized. They want positive feedback, and not just once a year at performance review time. My feeling is that once managers see that giving P&R is directly linked to performance, they'll see it as an integral part of their job—which is, after all, getting the best out of people—and start working to overcome these historical obstacles and objections.

In 1989 I had the pleasure of working with Jan Carlzon and a hundred of his top people at Scandinavian Airlines Systems (SAS) in Stockholm, Sweden. Carlzon, who stepped down as chairman of the airline in 1994, had turned around this bureaucracy—owned by Sweden, Norway, and Denmark—and made it into one of the best customer service organizations in Europe. When I was working with the SAS staff, I told them about what personal-growth guru Wayne Dyer says about the difference between ducks and eagles, and how Rick Tate, Gary Heil, and I use it in our Legendary Service program. When employees are ducks, they quack a lot and tell customers all the reasons why they can't serve them well: "It's our policy." "Don't blame me, I just work here." "The

computer's down." "You'll have to talk to the supervisor."
Quack, quack! Eagles, on the other hand, soar above the
crowd and do whatever it takes to serve the customer.

Carlzon loved hearing about this concept, particularly when I added my verbal shot at Employee of the
Month programs. What I believe in is Employee of the
Moment. In companies we work with, we set up an office
called the Eagle's Nest, and if anybody gets caught—by
either an internal or external customer—going the extra
mile, a call is immediately made to this office. The Eagle's
Nest dispatches someone with a Polaroid camera to see if
they can catch the eagle in flight. The person is recognized on the spot. Often a Wall of Fame is established,
where employees' pictures and eagle stories are displayed.

The day after working with Carlzon and his top
people, Margie and I were flying from Stockholm to
Rome to meet our kids, Scott and Debbie. We had
changed our reservations a number of times, so our travel
agent, Nada, arranged for us to pick up prepaid tickets
from Swiss Air. At the airport, we were instructed to
check in with SAS, since they handled the tickets and
baggage for all the airlines. Swiss Air had only a small
counter to deal with problems. When we went to the SAS
counter to check in, the agent asked for our tickets. I told
her we were there to pick up prepaid tickets. She told us,
"I normally don't deal with prepaid tickets. You'll have to
go to Swiss Air." Frustrated, I lowered my head and
started to mumble, "Where is Swiss Air?" (I was remembering the two-hour check-in we'd endured the previous
week, with another national airline. Employees had
seemed to take great pleasure in telling us we were in the
wrong line. They had run us all around the airport.)

At the time, a number of SAS customer service
employees had been trained to interpret nonverbal

communication cross-culturally. They had been told that if Americans lower their heads and start to mumble, they're probably getting upset. So our SAS agent smiled and said, "Why don't you two relax here? I'll go to Swiss Air." She walked from behind the desk, helped a couple behind us to enter another line, and headed out across the terminal. We couldn't believe it. When she got to Swiss Air, she went behind the counter to the computer and typed out our tickets. She waved our tickets to us as she started back, knowing we'd be watching. When she got back, she said, "Now I can check you in."

I asked, "What is your name?" She wanted to know why I was asking. When I traveled at that time, I carried postcards with me that had the One Minute Manager symbol on the back. If anyone treated me in a legendary fashion as this agent did, I immediately asked them for their name and their boss's name and address, and I sent their boss a card praising the employee. In this case, I pulled a card from my briefcase and wrote, "Dear Jan: I just caught your first Eagle of the Moment. Her name is Katrina Baugh, this is her department, and this is what she did for me." I signed my name and put the card in the airport mailbox.

Four days later I was in Rome and thought about Katrina. I called Jan Carlzon's office. I had met his secretary, and she told me Jan was out of the office. "Is there any way I can help you, Ken?" she asked.

"I just wanted to find out if Jan got my postcard."

"He sure did, and he went completely wild."

"What did he do?"

"He sent Katrina a letter. He sent her flowers. He wrote a story for our newsletter. And he threw a party in her honor in our office."

Can you imagine a top manager celebrating an employee who left her station? Who did she think she was? She thought she owned the place. And Carlzon agreed with her.

If I see somebody doing something casually that I don't think should be done casually, I don't hesitate to correct it on the spot. I can't let this creep into my football.

■ DON SHULA

SHULA

My philosophy is that there are no minor mistakes. If the team or an individual does something wrong, I or one of our staff will blow the whistle, tell them what they did wrong, and make them do it again. We do most of our redirecting during preseason training. Once the season starts, the players are expected to understand how to perform their roles. If they make any mistakes, we reprimand them. It's almost impossible for me to mask my feelings. If I'm upset, my players and coaches know it. I let all of my emotions out. My adrenaline flows, and everything just comes right out of me. But when I get upset with a player or the team, it is always focused on performance. Respect for my players is a given. I'm sometimes tough on our players, but they know I respect them as human beings. In my view, if I and my coaches just don't like one of our players or can't get along with him, he shouldn't be on our football team. This is why character is a very important part of my team selection. Sure, I want and need talented players, but if they don't have the character and kind of personality to fit in, they belong on another team.

I try to fit my feedback to a player's personality. Bob Griese, our great quarterback in the 1970s, was a very quiet, thoughtful person. He did not respond well to emotional reprimands. It was better to take him aside and talk to him quietly and in private. On the other hand, Dan Marino, our all-star quarterback today, is an emotional player and has to be treated in a completely different way. Consistency is key, but within this philosophy, you have to use different approaches.

Somehow, as a coach, you have to show that your standard for good performance is the one that the team has to follow. You usually do this within the routines of practice and play, by moving in to make corrections when performance is below your acceptable line. From time to time, some of the people you coach are going to test the limits. You have to pass these tests. You can't tolerate flagrant misbehavior or infractions of your rules. If you do, it sends the wrong message to the other players. But you must be wise in your confrontations and flexible in the way you treat people at such times. I've had some tense go-arounds with players in my time, and I know that when you're in this situation you can't walk away. This is another time when it's important to have your beliefs and standards clear and to have confidence in something bigger than your own ego.

During training camp in the summer of 1994, Tim Bowens, our big defensive tackle, was being razzed by the veterans at lunch. They always do that to the new guys. They wanted Tim to sing the Mississippi alma mater for the team. Bowens refused to sing. At 315 pounds, nobody was ready to make him, either. After lunch, when he went to dress for practice, he found that the veterans had completely cleaned out his locker. He had nothing in which to suit up for practice—the ultimate initiation for a rookie. Not understanding that they were only kidding, Bowens got into his car and drove back to his apartment in town.

Players are not allowed to leave training camp without permission, so Stu Weinstein, our security officer, went along with Bowens' agent to get him. They brought him back later in the afternoon and took him straight to my office. I said, "What happened, Tim?" He said, "Coach, I came here to play football, not sing." While I had to fine him for leaving camp, I tried to be very understanding of his situation. He was from a small town in Mississippi, had spent only one year at the university, and didn't quite understand the fun the other players were trying to have. He never left camp on his own again, and I'm sure glad. Bowens had a great rookie year. He was a key member of our defense and a leader of our pass rush. His contribution was important, and pleased Joe Greene and everyone on our staff.

■ DON SHULA

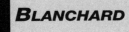
BLANCHARD

Redirecting is the way to correct a mistake when an individual or team has not yet learned to do what you want them to do. In other words, they have not yet done it well. If people make a mistake while they are learning and then you yell at them or punish them, you'll only increase their anxiety and motivate them to avoid the punisher—you. It's likely that people will get the wrong message if they're punished when they're learning something. (If, when your youngsters are learning to walk, you spank them every time they stumble, they're liable to be crawling to work when they're twenty-one.) When a learner makes a mistake, be sure the person knows that the behavior was incorrect, but take the blame upon yourself ("Maybe I didn't make it clear enough") and then patiently go back to the beginning and give redirection ("Let's review what we were going to do in the first place"). This means resetting the task parameters and, if possible, demonstrating what good behavior looks like.

A reprimand is an example of a negative consequence. You're telling people what they did wrong as soon as possible. A good reprimand is specific; it includes your feelings and ends by affirming the person. ("You didn't get your report in on time. It's frustrating to me because everyone else did. I'm upset because I normally can count on you.") Use a reprimand only when an individual or team has already proven that they can do what you want done, but are now falling short of it. To illustrate when to use redirection and when to give a reprimand, I'll use a story from my own coaching experience. When I was young and fast and thin, I was a basketball player. At one time I thought I would become a coach. When I was in college I had a chance to help coach the freshman teams. One year they'd recruited two big players. One guy from New York City was six-foot-six and could do it all. He could jump and run and shoot. He was one of the best players the college had recruited in a long time. The other kid was six-foot-nine and from upstate New York. If you threw him the ball and he caught it, it was considered progress. Why would you have a guy like this on the team? In the early 1960s big guys just weren't available, and often they were less coordinated than they are now. So if you found a guy who was six-foot-nine and could walk, you recruited him.

The only problem with the good player from the city was that he didn't like to play defense. He thought there was only one end of the court—where we had the ball on offense. We tried every way possible to get him to play defense. One night, finally, we reached our limit. When he was dogging it on defense, we called him out of the game; the head coach grabbed him by the shirt, threw him on the bench, and went nose-to-nose with him. We called him every name we could think of. His first response was to shout back, "Why are you yelling at me?" We'd never heard of a One-Minute Reprimand, but it just made sense to say, "Because you're good! You could be all-league if you just learned to play defense." After this, if he slowed down on defense, all we had to do was yell his name and he'd pick it up. He knew we'd call him out of the game and read him the riot act if he didn't.

If we had done that with the big guy from upstate, it would have immobilized him. He didn't know how to play defense, so he would have concluded we were unreasonable, and would probably have tried to retaliate or quit. When he had problems on defense, we'd call him out of the game and sit him down. We'd say, "John, the reason why that little kid you're guarding is getting all the rebounds is that whenever he shoots, you turn around and look up in the air like you're sightseeing in New York City. Then he runs around you, blocks you out, and grabs the rebound. Now, we're going to put you back in there. This time, when the other team shoots, we want you to imagine that there's nobody else in the world but your man, and we want you to watch him in a very special way. We want you to watch his belly button. Now, there's nothing dirty about that; research shows that where the belly button goes, the body follows."

When he went back in and the other team took a shot, he immediately focused his attention on the belly button of the man he was guarding. Seeing this big guy looking at his belly button, his opponent gazed down as if he wondered if his fly was open. Realizing that everything was intact, he began staring back at our big kid. While the two of them were staring at each other, neither was getting any rebounds. The opposing coach was yelling at his player and finally got his attention. With that, this player maneuvered Big John under the basket, where he was out of play to grab a rebound. So we called John out of the game and sat him down again. We told him, "That was a great belly button watch!" He laughed and said, "I never let it out of my sight."

We told him to go back into the game, but this time, while he was watching the opponent's belly button, to gradually turn around and face the basket, and if a rebound came off, to grab it. When we put John in the game, he did just that—and miraculously, the ball landed in his hands. Not knowing what to do with it, he turned around and faced his opponent, who knocked it out of his hands and laid it in for two points. When he returned to the bench, we said, "John, great belly button watch. Good turn too. This time, when the ball comes your way, grab it and hold on for dear life until you see a player wearing our uniform." Now, were we being mean to John? No. He just didn't know how to rebound. So every time we called him out of the game we were praising his progress and then redirecting his efforts for the next encounter. If we had done this with our good player from the city, he would have been insulted. He knew how to play defense; he just lacked motivation in the less dramatic parts of the game.

Whereas redirection is appropriate on a "can't do" problem—like our big guy's rebounding—a reprimand is in order if the matter is motivational, or "won't do" —like with our city kid's defense.

After delivering a reprimand, it's important for people to understand that you still value them as human beings. Make sure that the person you are confronting knows that you are upset because you expect more from him or her. ("You're better than this.") This step is so important, but sometimes it's difficult to do.

> When my son, Scott, was a senior in high school, he used to cause problems by parking his truck in the driveway. Nobody could get in or out because his truck was big enough to go to war. I told him to park it out in the street. One day I came home to find he'd not only blocked the driveway with his truck but had gone away and taken his keys with him. I was furious. Three hours later he showed up, and I was waiting for him. I stormed out of the house and I let him have it. I didn't leave him in doubt about what he'd done wrong and how I felt about it. As I was walking back to the house, Scott raced after me. He followed me into the kitchen. "Dad," he said, "You forgot the last part of the reprimand—you know, the part about, 'You're a good kid, I love you, and this is so unlike you.'" I cracked up laughing. We hugged. Scott never left his truck in the driveway again. And I became better at reaffirming at the end of a reprimand.
>
> ■ KEN BLANCHARD

HONESTY-BASED

Everything Don Shula does is honesty-based. *And this is exactly what people need and want in a leader today. Effective leaders are clear and straightforward in their interactions with others. If people can't have job security today, they want honesty. They want leaders to be straight with them. What you see in Don Shula is what you get.*

■ KEN BLANCHARD

Yes, Shula is just a pro football coach, albeit the best known by virtue of those 325 victories. But the fact is, in a place that lurches from day-to-day just waiting for the next scandal, Shula's single-minded plod after George Halas has rewarded him with a status that few public figures in south Florida can claim. He is clean.

■ S. L. PRICE, *MIAMI HERALD*,
SPECIAL SHULA EDITION,
NOVEMBER 15, 1993

SHULA

While I have gained recognition for my success as a coach, I am proudest when I am recognized for my integrity, an intangible that can't be measured by a win-loss record. For example, I felt good when journalist Peggy Stanton included me among nine men she profiled in her book *The Daniel Dilemma: The Moral Man in the Public Arena.* I was also proud when S. L. Price wrote—in the *Miami Herald,* the day after I broke the Halas record—that I was "clean."

Doing something unethical or dishonest would erode my self-esteem—my image of who I am as a person. If I did something that was not right, I would have trouble facing my family. I'll admit that football is a violent sport, but it's clean and it's tough. The struggle to succeed and the hard-fought nature of a win are to me all part of the American way of life. But there's no place in football for "unnecessary violence," as when a player deliberately hits an opponent in the head or clips him from behind. As a long-standing member of the NFL's Competition Committee, I have championed rules that decrease unnecessary rough play. If I'm remembered for anything as a coach, I hope it's for playing within the rules. I also hope it will be said that my teams showed class and dignity in victory or defeat. It is a source of pride that during my seasons with Miami, the Dolphins have been the least-penalized team in the NFL. When my team beats your team, I want it to be fair and square.

If our teams are to play by the rules, they must know them. This knowledge not only means we play "fair" but sometimes it can mean the difference between victory and defeat. Our last-second victory in December 1993 over the eventual Super Bowl champion Dallas Cowboys is a perfect example. The Cowboys were leading 16–14 when we made a great drive that set up a potential last-second winning field goal. When the field goal was blocked, it looked like the game was lost forever. This is when knowledge of the rules took over. All the Cowboys had to do was not touch the ball and the game was theirs. But when Leon Lett tried to pick up the ball for Dallas and it squirted from his hands, our unheralded offensive linemen Jeff Dellenbach and Bert Weidner knew the rule: when the Dallas player touched the ball, it had been reactivated. With this knowledge, they were there to pounce on the ball and help us retrieve victory from the jaws of defeat. When everything seemed lost, knowledge of the rules—and determination to figure a way to still win the game—prevailed. This is the way I like to see football played.

My concern for fairness makes me agonize over personnel decisions like whether to start Bob Griese, who was just coming back from a broken ankle, over Earl Morrall in the Super Bowl game against Washington during the 17–0 season. While Morrall had enabled us to get to the Super Bowl, he and the team had had trouble getting across the goal line the last game. In fact, Griese had started the second half of the Pittsburgh AFC championship game and engineered the victory. So, while Earl Morrall deserved to start for what he had done for the team in the past, I felt that it would not be fair to make a decision that was not in the best interest of the team. I went with Griese. It proved providential, as he led us to a 14–7 victory. But once I had made the decision, the question that bothered me was, How do you tell a guy who led you to eleven straight victories that he was not the fellow who would captain the biggest game of all?

Softening a blow is not one of my gifts. I approach things in a straightforward way—sit down and look the guy in the eye and say, "This is what I think. You may not agree with it. But this is the way I feel, and this is why I am doing it. I know it's tough to swallow, but I just want you to try to understand what I'm thinking and what my purpose is." The decision hurt Morrall, but he appreciated the way I handled it. In fact, he said, "The best thing that Don did was hit it head on. He didn't let anyone wonder all week who the quarterback would be, so people would choose up sides."

Don Shula not only values honesty in himself, he likes and respects it in others. In the last game of my first season as an NFL official, I made the worst call I'd ever made against Shula's Baltimore Colts. They were playing the Redskins in Baltimore, and the score was tied 17–17 when, in the waning minutes, Washington threw a pass into the end zone, and Rick Volk of the Colts intercepted it. On his third step, he hit a white line that I thought was the sideline. The line that Volk hit was actually a foot inside the end zone. Not knowing this at the time, I signaled a touchback as Volk raced down the field on a touchdown run of 106 yards, a run that would have broken a record that had stood since 1920. I compounded my mistake by chasing Volk down the field to get the ball. Shula and the whole Baltimore team were furious with me. A few plays later, after I'd realized my mistake, I passed by the Baltimore bench and Shula hollered, "Hey, rookie, what the hell are you doing out there?" I stopped and said, "Coach, I blew it, and I feel terrible about it."

After the game, which Baltimore lost, the reporters gathered around Shula and immediately wanted to know what he thought about my call. Shula said, "Holst came by the bench and told me that he blew it and that he felt badly. He's an honest man. Next question."

ART HOLST, FORMER NFL OFFICIAL

BLANCHARD

In 1994 *Fortune* magazine featured a story called "The New Deal in Business." The old deal was that if an employee gave a company loyalty, the company would guarantee this person job security. According to the article, nobody can live by this agreement any more. Job security is a thing of the past, and so is loyalty. What's the new deal? In working with companies across the country, we've been trying to find that out. When we ask managers what they want from their employees, they tell us initiative, problem solving, and willingness to take responsibility—everything that people talk about when they refer to "empowered" employees. When we ask employees what they want from management, more than anything else they say they want honesty—they want to be told the truth. They don't want to be told there'll be no more layoffs, and then two months later have exactly that. They want it the Shula way—straight.

In a competitive environment, where it seems anything goes, ethical considerations are often the first to be abandoned. The reason this doesn't work is that the number one characteristic people are looking for in a leader is integrity.

John Wooden, the great UCLA basketball coach, said it well: "There is no pillow as soft as a clear conscience." The greatest payoff for being totally honest with others is self-esteem. If this is true, why aren't more people ethical? One of the reasons that being ethical is often a low priority is that there is an unfounded belief that it might not be best for business. The exact opposite is true. In working on our book *The Power of Ethical Management,* Norman Vincent Peale and I found evidence that being ethical does, in fact, make good business sense—financially and otherwise. Companies that are successful over the long term tend to be ethical companies.

Good business focuses on developing and maintaining long-term relationships. A company that makes a quick financial gain by taking advantage of customers, suppliers, or employees may show a slightly higher profit this quarter. But the trust that was lost in the process may never be restored. Disgruntled customers will switch to a competitor as soon as it's convenient. A supplier that was taken advantage of will find a way to gain the upper hand. And employees who feel they are treated unfairly will even the score with their employer by stealing supplies or inventory, padding expense accounts, making personal long-distance phone calls while at work, calling in sick on days when they are well, and so forth.

Astute business managers know that business success and ethical practices go hand in hand. They have a broader focus on the purpose of business, a focus that supersedes the daily activities. They know that, ultimately, there is no right way to do a wrong thing. Kenneth T. Derr, chairman of Chevron Corporation, says: "There's no doubt in my mind that being ethical pays, because I know that, in our company, people who sleep well at night work better during the day."

I don't know how to play games with people. My feelings are on my sleeve. When I'm happy, I'm happy. When I'm upset, I'm upset. I'm honest and straight with my people and I want them to be honest and straight with me.

■ DON SHULA

SHULA

At my first press conference after I came to Miami, I was asked to describe my style. I said, "I'm about as subtle as a punch in the mouth." I have a straight-up approach. I don't know how to go around corners or how to finesse. My players know this and they expect candor from me. Congruence is important to me. What you see with Don Shula is what you get. I don't play games. Effective coaches confront their people, praise them sincerely, redirect or reprimand them without apology, and above all are honest with them. Integrity pays, and integrity means being honest with yourself and others. This is a key ingredient in my coaching philosophy.

For example, if we have a player who is not living up to his potential, giving everything that he has to be the best that he can be, I think this situation has to be confronted straight-on. I want to solve this problem as soon as I can, rather than let it fester. This is why, in the spring of 1994, I sat down man-to-man with Keith Jackson, the great free agent tight end whom we had acquired from the Philadelphia Eagles in 1992. In Jackson's first year with us, he made a real contribution. But during the 1993–94 season, he didn't play much because of minor injuries. When he did play, he never got back into shape or played the way he was capable of playing. If we wanted a chance at the Super Bowl in 1995, we couldn't afford to be without the important leadership of Jackson. He's a calming influence who is able to take victory and defeat in stride and model important things for our younger players. By talking to Jackson in an honest way and expecting him be honest with me, I hoped to leave the 1993–94 season behind us. Keith seemed to appreciate this. He knew I wouldn't be talking to him if I didn't respect his talent and capabilities and who he was as a human being. At least, I hope he did.

I strive to make sure that what I say and what I do are the same. I've learned a lot over the years and am not quite as intense and emotional as I used to be. But I hope my players have learned I mean what I say and say what I mean. To me that kind of congruence is the foundation for effective coaching. No matter what situation you are in, coaching others will require new things of you. It will give you opportunities to grow. Dealing with others in a leadership capacity will test your character, especially if your role is a highly visible one. You should expect the pressures and be ready for them by becoming as clear as you can about what you believe, what's good enough for you, and how you need to treat people in order to get the job done.

BLANCHARD

Most people have had the experience of driving a car without remembering to release the emergency brake. You can't figure out what's holding the car back. When you discover the problem and let the brake off, the car jumps ahead. There's a brake like this on in organizations today, and it has to do with the difference between what managers say they stand for and how they actually treat people. A huge amount of energy is lost in organizations by having people complaining and commiserating over the lack of congruence in company leaders.

I've been working during the past few years with Michael O'Connor—an author and leading consultant in the field of organizational values—helping organizations "manage by values" by finding and closing the gaps between what they stand for and how they behave. To what extent does management walk its talk? Once we know what kind of vision an organization and its leaders have, we can examine the management practices in this organization to see if they are aligned with the vision.

In the Managing By Values (MBV) process our company teaches, congruence is a key factor. In each of the MBV companies with which we've worked, ethics is the number-one value. Once their mission and their operating values were established and communicated to everyone, these organizations needed a process for closing gaps between what the company stood for and its management practices and routine behavior. If a manager yells at someone for not doing something and then storms out of the area, the person who has been yelled at is encouraged to call out, "Gap!" (One aspect of being ethical is not eroding someone else's self-esteem.) The manager and the employee then sit down and do what we call a POPS (People-Oriented Problem Solving). They use a set of questions designed to guide them through an analysis of the problem and through the development of a plan to prevent its reoccurrence. If the employee is hesitant to confront his or her boss, the employee can request that an elected company ombudsman facilitate the POPS session. This gap-closing system brings congruence between the shared values and organizational behavior. We've designated those organizations that are attempting to close these behavioral gaps by managing by values as being on a "Fortunate 500" journey.

More than a hundred companies send me their annual reports every year. Each report opens with statements like "Without our customers, we'd be nothing," and "Our employees are our most important resource." Apparently everybody thinks that customers and employees are important. But what do we find when we look at how these companies treat their customers and people? Gap City. For example, what happens when a customer has a problem? Most organizations put customers under a hot lamp and interrogate them. This is why most customers don't complain—they just take their business elsewhere.

I was visiting my nephew Steve Dann in New Jersey and needed to rent a car. I went to the major rental agency our company uses. We're not the biggest contract they have, but for us it's sizable. Now, I'd goofed and left my driver's license in California, so I asked my nephew to give me his license. The trouble began when I put Steve's license and my credit card down in front of the agent. The guy sniffed at them and announced triumphantly, "License and credit card have to have the same name on them."

I got a credit card from Steve and put it on the counter. The agent looked at them, and then at Steve and asked, "How old are you?"

"Twenty-four."

"You have to be twenty-five to rent a car in metropolitan New York."

Taken aback, I said, "Can't you look in your computer? My company has an account with you. I'm sure you'll find my license number in there."

"Listen," the guy said with a stern look, "if you want to rent a car, bring a license. Next!"

Now I recognize that you need to have your license on you when you rent a car, but this guy was a customer service nightmare.

Contrast this with the treatment Steve and I had received on an earlier trip to Syracuse from a small regional outfit, which I use whenever I'm in that town. When I told the agent I'd left my license in California, she smiled and said, "Don't worry about it, Dr. Blanchard. I've already entered your license number in the computer. By the way, it's not up for renewal until May 1995. Let's sign up your nephew as a driver."

Why was this small company so different? Apparently, the outfit in Newark hadn't read the signs they'd put up all over about the importance of the customer.

Gaps are a problem not only in our organizations, they're a problem in our personal lives. We say our family is important, yet the average couple in America is reported to talk to each other only seven minutes a day, and the average household has the TV on an average of five to six hours a day. We say our health is important, yet when do most people begin a good exercise or nutrition program? When they have a heart attack. All of us must find ways of bridging the gaps between what we say and what we do. What inspires me about working with Don Shula is his striving for congruence, not only in his organizational life but in his personal life.

Football is a serious game with a lot of money at stake, people's jobs and their pride. But there's also a sense of humor. I recall the first time I wore glasses to referee an NFL game. On our way to the field, the other six officials and I passed John Madden, who was coaching Oakland at the time. He looked at me and said, "Two hundred million people in this country, and we can't even find seven without glasses?" Everyone, including myself, broke up.

■ ART HOLST, FORMER NFL OFFICIAL

SHULA

I'm called all kinds of names—Sherman Tank, Bulldozer, and others. Everyone talks about my jutting jaw and the fact that I once said, "I don't get ulcers, I give them." But there are few things I like better than a good laugh. A sense of humor helps you keep things in perspective. If I am blunt and honest with someone on our team, I hope this person keeps things in perspective and realizes that I am trying to bring out the best in him and do what is best for the team. A sense of humor also permits you to accept criticism without getting consumed by it. Criticism never becomes a life-and-death situation. One of my greatest joys in coaching has been working with players who had a good sense of humor. They took what they did seriously—but they took themselves lightly. They also helped me do the same.

Hall of Famer Larry Csonka was this kind of guy. I have known few people who were as competitive and who showed as much leadership on the field as Csonka. He was a fierce competitor and gave 150 percent. He expected everyone else to do the same. Csonka is the only guy I've ever seen who got called for unnecessary roughness on offense. He was running with the ball along the sideline when an opposing tackler approached him. When Csonka saw the tackler coming, he unloaded with a huge forearm and knocked him out of bounds. As Csonka continued down the field, a flag was thrown. I ran up to the official and asked what the penalty was for.

"Unnecessary roughness," I was told.

"By the tackler?" I wondered.

"No! By your ball carrier."

While Csonka loved to play in the games, he was not always as excited about practice. Our staff sometimes had to motivate him in practice. In the press, Csonka and his buddy Jim Kiick were known as Butch Cassidy and the Sundance Kid. One time I got on them during the perfect season. I was riding them both pretty hard. I went to take a shower after practice, and when I opened the door, I found a live alligator staring me in the face! I jumped back and ran out of the shower room— straight to Csonka's locker.

"What are you guys doing?" I yelled.

Csonka smiled and said, "Don't yell at us, Coach. You should thank Jim and me, instead. The rest of the team wanted the alligator's mouth left open, but we voted to have it taped."

Another story I like to tell is about Jimmy Orr, the gifted receiver I coached at Baltimore. Orr was great at catching passes, but he didn't like to block downfield. His reluctance to get physical annoyed me. One day I decided to confront the problem in front of the entire squad. To make my point, I talked about all the great runs Jimmy Brown, the legendary Cleveland Browns fullback, was making. I said, "If you study Cleveland's films, every time Brown makes a long run, he has receivers like Ray Renfrew downfield throwing key blocks for him. These blocks are what enable him to score or gain big yardage. And yet here we've got a receiver who won't hit anybody. Orr, you could at least get downfield and get into somebody's way."

Orr said, "Coach, before you go on, could I say something?"

"Sure," I said.

"You can't expect a thoroughbred to do a mule's work."

This really broke me up. In the middle of a serious point, Orr had brought me to my knees. Over the years, I've learned that the ideal way to be is working hard and accomplishing while enjoying what you're doing. This helps create an honest and open environment.

Some of the most frequent recipients of Shula's temper—and of his humor—have been the referees. "Shula's a very intense guy," says Art Holst, a former NFL official who's been around the coach for years. "He called me an _____ for years," Holst smiles. "One time, on a Pittsburgh punt, he felt Pittsburgh was offside. I disagreed. Later in the game Miami completed a pass and I called clipping. Shula was following me down the field yelling, 'Come over here, _____ ! I want to talk to you, _____ !'

"I said, 'What do you want, Coach?'

"'I want to talk to you about your missing that movement in the line and then calling a clip on us. That was no clip!'

"I said, 'You know me, Coach. I've been in the league for eight years, and I'll call anything I see. I don't call what I can't see.'

"Shula turned around and walked away four or five steps. Then he turned back and smiled and said, 'Okay, Art, you're right. But you're still an _____ !' We both laughed."

Former NFL Official Jim Tunney laughs when you mention Don Shula's name. "Shula knows the rules so well that officials sometimes see him as intimidating. My favorite Shula story is this: I'm working a Dolphins-Redskins game in Washington, and we have a rookie field judge. There's a pass by the Dolphins, and it looks like there is interference twenty-five yards down the field, but the judge doesn't call it. Shula starts yelling at me, 'Tunney! Tunney! What's going on here?' I was out of position and can't make the call, so it is the field judge's opinion that has to count. So I go down and ask the field judge how he saw that last third-down pass play. 'Jim,' he says, 'there was contact, but they were both going for the ball.' I say, 'So in your judgment there was no interference,' and he says, 'Right. Do you want me to go over and tell Coach Shula?' I laugh and say, 'If you did that now, I figure that would be quite a little orientation program for you. No way am I going to send you over there!'

"So I go over to talk to Shula, and he's three or four yards onto the field. The coaches aren't supposed to be out there, but Shula tends to forget where the lines are sometimes. He starts yelling at me right away, and I say, 'Back up, Coach. Back up, Coach.' Finally I get him on the sideline. I put my hands behind my back, assume an authoritarian look, and say, 'Can I help you now, Coach?' He says, 'That was pass interference. That defender was banging our receiver and there's no doubt about it!' I say quietly, 'I just talked to the field

> *judge, and he said that there was contact but it was equal opportunity.*
> *There was no interference.' Shula says, 'Tunney, you've been screwing me*
> *for eighteen years!' I say, 'No, Coach, I think it's nineteen.' He laughs and*
> *I laugh, and it's all over."*
>
> ■ KEN BLANCHARD

BLANCHARD

My mother always said that I laughed before I cried, sang before I spoke, and danced before I walked. I was always a happy kid. Laughter was part of my growing up, but there also came a time when I realized that humor could also be helpful in stressful situations and even play an important part in leadership development. I had an interesting upbringing. In New Rochelle, New York, I attended an elementary school that was 95 percent Jewish. On Jewish holidays, they put all of us Gentile kids in a single classroom; this is how few of us there were. In my sixth-grade year, we entered a city-wide elementary basketball tournament and got into the finals against an elementary school that was 95 percent black. The other school had a big kid on their team by the name of Earl Forte. All of his teammates called him Meatball. He was head and shoulders above the rest of us.

I was always a pretty good shooter, and that day I had one of those games that you dream about—almost everything I threw up went in. We won, and after the game, I went to change my clothes. As I went by the locker where Earl was sitting I said, "Nice game, Meatball!" He whipped around, grabbed me by the shirt, and threw me against the locker. "Only my friends call me Meatball!" he shouted. I don't know where I got the composure as a young kid, but I laughed and said, "Oh, then why don't we become friends?" He cracked up and put me down and said, "You're okay." After graduation, these same two elementary schools merged into a junior high school. When I became a successful candidate for seventh-grade class president, Earl became one of my campaign managers. He and I remained good friends throughout our schooling together.

I think people in organizations today take themselves too seriously. They all seem to have tight underwear on. A fun smile or a really good laugh is hard to find within most organizational walls. It's hard to be honest and forthright with folks whose egos and pride are always up for grabs. Feedback is the breakfast of champions, but it can only be given effectively in an environment where people don't feel they have to defend themselves all the time. Where does a sense of humor start? With yourself. What we need to do is laugh at ourselves first. We are, after all, pretty funny creatures. In celebrating every major birthday I have, our company roasts me. They have a great time portraying my idiosyncrasies, through skits and other activities. Margie says, "I guess I'm married to a real character." On my fortieth birthday, my mother was in town for the festivities. When everyone started to laugh and make fun of me, she turned and said to me, "If you're in charge here, why is everyone laughing?" The reality is, I've always been proud that people feel comfortable enough to poke fun at me. This sets a tone in our company that doesn't let us take ourselves too seriously.

Whenever I feel I'm taking myself too seriously, I have a morning skip. I used to jog, but my knee started bothering me. People told me to walk, but I found that it wasn't strenuous enough. Some years back, I talked to a doctor who'd served on the Olympic Medical Committee. He suggested I skip. He said it was more aerobic than walking and less injurious than running because you always have one foot on the ground. You should see the expressions I get from drivers when I come skipping up the street. The thing about skipping is that you can't do it without laughing yourself. Who likes to skip? Kids. A friend of mine, Tom Crum, who wrote *The Magic of Conflict*, has worked a lot with young people, teaching martial arts. He says that when he works with little kids, he never asks for volunteers, because the whole group will stand up. Nobody's told them yet that they can make fools of themselves. When he works with high school kids, he has to handpick his volunteers ahead of time. Everybody's worried about not looking good.

It's the same when a little kid swings a golf club. What does he do if he misses? He laughs and calls all his friends over. But when an adult swings and misses the ball, the person is horrified and looks around to see if anybody has been watching. We seem to stifle the child in ourselves and in others. As Tom Crum says, we start living from a perspective of judgment rather than discovery. When all the emphasis in business is on whether we're doing things right or wrong, we never get to experience the delight you have when you exclaim, "Isn't that interesting!" Crum also teaches a course called The Magic of Skiing in Aspen every winter. When his students are careening down the slopes, about to fall, he has them shout out, "YES!" with a great grin on their face. It's amazing how lightly you fall compared with a skier who's trying to look good and is grimacing with tension as the unwelcome tumble approaches. It's also amazing how this childlike attitude toward falling helps prevent injuries, which are so often the result of tension in the muscles.

Grimacers in organizations get hurt trying to look good, too. It happens every day. I once was on a program with Norman Cousins, author of *Anatomy of an Illness*. He said, "If you ever get sick, don't go to a hospital. The food is lousy, the TVs are way up at the ceiling where you strain your neck, and they keep waking you up to give you shots. Go to a good hotel that has excellent room service and hire nurses and doctors to come on *your* schedule." When Cousins got cancer, he did just that and then refused to see any visitor unless the person brought a funny movie or had some good jokes to tell him. The Marx Brothers and the Three Stooges were his favorites. His laughter cured him of cancer and made him a leader in the healing power of humor.

One of the joys of watching Don Shula and the Miami Dolphins is that, while they're serious about winning, on the practice field, in the locker room, and on the sidelines, humor plays an important part. It makes wins extra special and helps heal the occasional wound of defeat.

My goal in life is to be an applied behavioral scientist. I want to take the BS out of the behavioral sciences and make what we know about people come alive so it can be useful to everyone.

■ KEN BLANCHARD

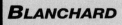
BLANCHARD

Well, that's it. Those are Don Shula's five secrets of effective coaching, and my organizational twist on them. I think our country needs more leaders who:

1. Stand for something—they are CONVICTION-DRIVEN.
2. Are willing to roll up their sleeves and do whatever it takes to accomplish established goals. They believe in OVERLEARNING through perfect practice.
3. Have a game plan but are willing to adjust or change when circumstances dictate. They are action focused but AUDIBLE-READY.
4. Are predictable in their response to performance. They praise, redirect, and reprimand appropriately, because they are CONSISTENT over time.
5. Are clear and straightforward in their interactions with others. Everything they do is HONESTY-BASED.

Now that you've read about our philosophy of coaching and seen how it applies in various settings other than football, you are ready to look in the mirror and assess your own coaching effectiveness. There are two parts of this assessment: reflecting on the past and planning for the future.

Whenever I get to spend time with a winner and learn about this person's secrets of success, I find myself *reflecting on the past*. Personal experiences of failure and success flash through my mind.

A FAILURE EXPERIENCE

As I began to learn about Shula's approach to coaching, I recalled my first teaching assignment at Ohio University. Fresh out of graduate school, I'd been hired as administrative assistant to the dean of the Business School. Harry Everts, my boss, wanted all his assistants to teach at least one course; he assigned me to the management department and asked the department chairman, Paul Hersey, to give me a class to teach. I had never anticipated teaching. All my professors in graduate school had told me I could never be a college professor because my writing wasn't academic enough. (This, I learned later, meant that a reader could understand my writing.) I had to develop a teaching strategy fast. As a student, I'd always rebelled against the authoritarian style of teaching. So I decided to be humanistic. The first day of class, I told the students, "I'm Ken Blanchard, your teacher for this course. Call me Ken. We're going to teach this course together. Don't worry about grades—you'd have to work at it to make less than an *A*."

I went on to tell the students how exciting the course was going to be: "But if you'd rather spend time elsewhere where you have more interest, by all means do it. Come to class if you want to participate in the learning process. If you choose not to participate, at the end of the course, I'll give you an exam based on the book. Your performance on this test will constitute your grade." After making this statement, I suggested that those who just wanted to take the test at the end of the course could leave. To my amazement, in a matter of minutes, the size of that class went from 110 students to just 8. They almost knocked me down as they went out the door yelling, "We found one!" They told all their friends about this easy course they were in, and there were so many sign-ups for the class that they had to close registration for it. The next semester, the dean wouldn't list my name as the instructor of this course in the catalogue because every student would have wanted in. My boss gave me a lecture on the merits of classroom control. I became known as a "rate buster"—one whose grading practices upset the carefully maintained averages of the others. It was said I was trying to get too close to students. When I got on an elevator, faculty members would look the other way. I was popular with the students, but I had no respect from either them or the faculty. When the final exam was given, performance was far below standards. The students didn't know the material. Can you imagine what Don Shula would have said to me if I was one of his assistant coaches and pulled this kind of thing? I certainly didn't C.O.A.C.H. to win.

A SUCCESS EXPERIENCE

A number of years back, my good friend Carlos Arbelaez and I agreed to coach our sons' youth soccer team. Youth sports in our southern California community is a very big deal. For example, every league begins with a drafting night, when coaches meet and determine what players will be on each team. They draw numbers and pick players in a predetermined order just like in the NFL and NBA. Neither Carlos nor I could attend the drafting event, so we told the league organizers to have someone pick our team, which was to include our sons David and Scott. Among a group of ten- to twelve-year-old boys with mixed skills, we were given two very good players. We quickly learned, however, that the other coaches had rejected these two boys because they were discipline problems.

As soon as we received our roster, we called the parents and boys and invited them to a meeting at my home. At this meeting, we told the parents, "We want to share with you our vision for the team so you can decide whether you want your son to play for us or not." They were confused by this because they had assumed that their sons would be on our team just by showing up. We explained that Carlos (who had played soccer in college) would be in charge of the athletic coaching, while I would manage the human aspect of the team. We told them that there were four roles in the game of soccer: (1) there were players, who wore shorts and played; (2) there were coaches, who walked up and down on the sidelines; (3) there were referees who had striped shirts and blew whistles; and (4) there were parents, who sat in the stands and cheered.

We made it clear that we didn't want anybody to get any of these roles confused. The boys, for instance, would not be allowed to referee. The parents would not referee, either, and neither would they be invited to coach the team. They certainly were too old to play. What would help us tremendously was everybody being clear about his or her role and how we were going to operate.

Once the roles were squared away, we moved on to our vision for the team. We shared four learning goals that we had for the boys. We wanted to teach them:

1. Skills—Carlos was an experienced soccer player and eager to teach the boys the fundamentals of the game.

2. Teamwork and cooperation—Soccer is not an individual sport, so the boys would learn how to work together as a team.
3. Good sportsmanship—We felt that this was an important lesson for boys to learn as early as possible. At their age, winning was not as important as how they played the game.
4. Enjoyment—Sometimes having fun gets lost in youth competition sports. Since our players were kids first and players second, we wanted them to enjoy themselves and have fun.

A parent raised his hand and asked, "What about winning?" I replied, "Winning is an outgrowth of doing these four things. If we can teach the boys some skills, teamwork and cooperation, good sportsmanship, and have fun at the same time, the Santos [our team] will win a number of games. However, we want to make it clear that we are unwilling to sacrifice any of these four learning goals in an effort to win."

Carlos and I got specific about what we meant. If a good player acted like a poor sport, this player would get to rest on the sidelines. If a player wanted to be an individual showboat and not work as a team player, this boy would be out of there for a while, too. We would make sure that everyone would get to play an equal amount of time. If more experienced players wanted to win, it would be their job to coach and help the learners. This was going to be a complete team effort. A number of the parents and boys seemed skeptical, but they all agreed, in the end, to go along with our philosophy.

After the meeting, we told Kevin and Mike—the two talented but "challenging" boys—that we wanted to talk to them before practice began. We arranged to have them meet us the next day at Baskin-Robbins, a popular ice-cream parlor. When they arrived, we could tell they expected us to read them the riot act. So we caught them completely off balance when we said, "We're so happy about having you on our team. We've heard what good players you both are. We'd like to make you our assistant coaches." The boys' eyes lit up in disbelief.

In our practice sessions before the league games started, Carlos designed fun drills to teach the boys the fundamentals of the game, on both offense and defense: kicking, passing, dribbling, blocking, etc. Often he would use Kevin and Mike to demonstrate. He and I would observe the kids and then praise progress, as well as redirect efforts. We wanted to make sure that the players had their basic skills down. In a few practices, we were able to determine which boys would be best at which positions.

As we moved closer to the first game, Carlos began to emphasize teamwork and how each position contributed to the entire Santos effort. We arranged a couple of scrimmages so the less-experienced players could get some game time in before league play began. Once the competition began, I wrote a weekly Santos newsletter that summarized the game just played, and praised the team effort and the contribution of each of the boys. My praisings were very specific in terms of what we were working on as a team as well as individually. I ended each newsletter commenting on areas of improvement for each boy and for the team. The letter was written in an upbeat tone, and was sent to the homes of the boys so both they and their parents could read it. Everyone thought it helped keep our original goals in mind and made people feel like they were a part of the program.

I had a lesson in adaptability and making use of our team's resources. Carlos, my coaching partner and the soccer brains of our dynamic duo, couldn't make our most important game of the year. He had business responsibilities that took him out of town. So far, we were undefeated, but we were playing against the best coach in the league and another undefeated team. I was concerned, to say the least. Human relations I knew about, soccer I didn't. But as I drove up to the field, there waiting for me were Kevin and Mike, our two assistant coaches. You remember, the discipline problems. They said, "Mr. Blanchard! We thought you might be nervous about the game, so we wanted to reassure you that everything is under control." During the game, our kids played their hearts out, with Mike and Kevin calling the shots. With less than three minutes to play, we broke a 1–1 tie with a goal. Immediately Mike and Kevin switched places with two defensive players. This confused me, so I called Mike and Kevin over and said, "What's going on here?"

Mike said, "We're just putting our speed at defense now so we can protect our lead."

"That sounds great," I said with a smile. I don't know what I would have done without them. They knew what to change and what to do. The long and the short of the story is that we went undefeated and we won the league. We never once compromised our vision or convictions. Our team turned out to be a tightly knit unit including the parents, the kids, and the coaches. I think Don Shula would have been proud of us. All aspects of the C.O.A.C.H. acronym were in operation.

Learning is defined as a change in behavior. You haven't learned a thing until you can take action and use it.

■ DON SHULA AND KEN BLANCHARD

SHULA & BLANCHARD

"Who believed in you?" asked a management seminar leader. One participant shared his story. "When I was a teenager I took care of mowing the neighbor's lawn. When they got ready to go on a three-week vacation, they told me they were leaving me in charge of the whole place. When they gave me the house key, I felt something I'd never felt before. They believed in me, and that made me want to do the best job I could. And I did."

Who believed in you? Don had Paul Brown as his football mentor and coach. Ken Blanchard had his Miss Symmes, who saw his potential as a writer. Perhaps someone did or said something that gave you a positive shock of recognition about yourself. That person's vision of what you were capable of ignited something inside you. You said to yourself, "Well, if they think I can do it, maybe I can." You were challenged to reach down into yourself and call forth the effort that matched their vision of your potential. Lo and behold, you rose to it!

The question is: How do you create that spark of self-recognition in others? In your life you'll have coaching opportunities that are expected. They appear as a natural function of your designated role as a manager, as a parent, as a Little League coach or Girl Scout leader. The secrets in this book will help you rise to these challenges.

When Heather Whitestone won the 1994 Miss America contest, attention focused on her background. How did a girl who was deaf since birth surpass all the other beautiful and talented contestants to earn this coveted award? Heather's secret was the belief and faith shown in her by her mother, Daphne Gray, who steadfastly refused to see her daughter's deafness as a handicap.

Daphne's belief that Heather could be anything she wanted to be was transferred to the girl, who then went on to become a peak performer. This modern-day success story echoes another well-known one: Helen Keller's teacher took someone who by society's standards at the time should have been a throw-away person, and planted and nurtured the seed of belief that anything was possible. Helen then became a woman of wisdom and an example to people everywhere.

So your roles will furnish you with naturally occurring opportunities to coach others. But don't stop there. Other chances to recognize people's potential will present themselves every day, everywhere you go—provided you keep your eyes open. When Norman Vincent Peale celebrated his 90th birthday at the Waldorf Astoria, people rose one by one to tell how important Norman had been in their lives. When the guest of honor stood up to speak, he shared an anecdote that typifies his whole life as a spiritual coach to millions. In his speech, Norman said:

> On a recent plane trip I noticed that the businessman sitting next to me was looking worried. I decided to engage him in conversation.
>
> "How are you doing?" I asked
>
> "Oh, not so good," was the reply.
>
> "What's wrong?"
>
> "I just got promoted."
>
> "What's so bad about that?
>
> "I'm just not sure I've got what it takes to do the job."
>
> "Yes, you do."
>
> "Why, how do you know?"
>
> "You do—if you *think* you do!"

Then I told him to start each day chanting, "*Think* big! *Act* big! *Be* big! *Think* big! *Act* big! *Be* big!" By the time we had landed, that man was in a different frame of mind.

There it is. You can even be a coach to a total stranger! One entry point, one teachable moment presents itself, and you step in. It may happen in a conversation with a neighbor's child or a friend's relative or an employee of someone else that you plant the seed. When something draws you to a person, trust that feeling. Share your vision, like Norman did. You may be creating a turning point in that person's life. For the real difference in coaching is not about talent. Or personality. Or pride. Or ambition. It's about you believing in someone. And then doing whatever it takes to help that person be his or her very best.

SKILL DEVELOPMENT

Reading about Don Shula's philosophy of coaching can be useful for reanalyzing the past, both successes and failures. But there's another aspect of self-assessment. This involves *planning the future* by analyzing how your present coaching approach stacks up against Shula's game plan secrets. Once this is done, then you can determine how you can put what you have learned from this book into action on a day-to-day basis as you try to help people be their best.

On the following pages there is a score sheet for you to keep. It will help you set goals for improving your coaching. It will also enable you to track your progress.

Each of the five secrets in the C.O.A.C.H. acronym is presented below. The secret is then broken out into a series of more specific points. After each of these points is a series of questions. These are included to help you determine how your performance in this area can be assessed. If you can't answer a question, this might suggest an area for improvement.

After reading each set of questions, go back to the main point and indicate whether you think this area is a *strength* of yours or whether it is an area in your coaching approach that *needs improvement.* You can plot your current performance in this skill or principle in terms of the extent to which you see yourself employing it in your coaching of others.

You can institute a continuous self-improvement plan for your coaching by doing the following:

1. Rate yourself in all areas now. This provides a baseline for improvement.
2. Select one or two areas you want to work on. Practice in these areas for a few weeks. Then assess yourself again in this area.
3. Pick another specific goal for improvement, and practice some more. Work through each area.
4. Give this Score Sheet to those around you and ask them to give you some feedback (anonymously, if necessary) on these coaching principles. Then, at a future date, ask them to give you feedback a second time to see if their perceptions of you have changed.

SCORE SHEET

CONVICTION-DRIVEN

1. Articulate a vision. (please check)

   Strength _____ Needs improvement _____

   - What is your vision for your organization, department, team, or family?

   - What convictions drive your vision?

   - What kind of team are you building? How clearly have you communicated your vision?

   - How important is fun in your game plan?

2. Keep winning and losing in perspective.

   Strength _____ Needs improvement _____

   - What does success mean to you?

- What does failure mean to you?

- When you lose, do you merely mourn the loss, or do you turn it into an opportunity by learning from it?

- How good are you at moving on after a disappointment?

3. Lead by example.

   Strength _____ Needs improvement _____

   - What kind of example do you set for those you coach?

   - Do you ask people to do things you yourself won't do?

   - How much extra time and effort are you willing to put in?

   - Are you committed or only interested?

4. Value respect more than popularity.

   Strength _____ Needs improvement _____

   • How important is it for you to be liked?

   • How do you share yourself with your team members?

   • What qualities or actions do you think your people respect you for?

   • What do you want your team to remember you for?

5. Prize character as well as ability.

   Strength _____ Needs improvement _____

   • What do you look for in the people you choose for your team?

   • Which is more important to you, talent or character?

   • Are your choices determined more by the short run or the long run?

6. Enjoy what you do.

   Strength _____ Needs improvement _____

   • What would you work hard at for no pay?

   • Are you glad when your coaching is over or when it begins?

   • Is coaching a task or a source of satisfaction for you?

OVERLEARNING

1. Limit the number of player-development goals.

   Strength _____ Needs improvement _____

   • How many things do you have your performers working on at any one time?

   • How do you build in self-monitoring and self-correction?

   • How do you make sure that the most important things are the most urgent to your team members?

2. Make people master assignments.

Strength _____ Needs improvement _____

- How rigorous are you as a coach about making people know their assignments?

- What part does being on autopilot play in your team's performance?

3. Reduce practice errors.

Strength _____ Needs improvement _____

- How important are "practice errors" to you?

- How carefully do you monitor your team's performance?

- What sort of teaching plan do you follow?

4. Practice continuous improvement.

Strength _____ Needs improvement _____

- How important is it to you, as a coach, that your people keep on learning?

- How open are you yourself to learning? To changing what isn't working?

- How concerned are you about closing gaps between your professed values and your actual coaching practice?

AUDIBLE-READY

Strength _____ Needs improvement _____

- How flexible are you?

- Do you sometimes let your ego—your need to be right or to win—control your decision making?

- How open are you to suggestions from others?

- To what extent do you train those you coach to be ready to change the plan?

CONSISTENCY

1. Manage consequences.

   Strength _____ Needs improvement _____

   - How carefully do you monitor people's performance so you can manage consequences appropriately?

   - Are you consistent?

   - Do you behave the same way in similar circumstances—praise good performance, redirect or reprimand for less than standard results?

2. Provide positive consequences.

   Strength _____ Needs improvement _____

   - How important is praising to you as a coaching strategy?

   - How good are you at catching people doing things right, and giving them an appropriate pat on the back?

   - Are your praisings timely? Specific? Self-disclosing in terms of your feelings?

- When someone is learning, do you wait until they do it exactly right before you praise the person or do you recognize progress?

3. Redirect.

   Strength _____ Needs improvement _____

   - Do you stop and redirect when a person's performance is incorrect?

   - Do you treat an error from a beginner differently than a similar mistake from a good performer?

4. Provide negative consequences.

   Strength _____ Needs improvement _____

   - How willing are you to reprimand people when they "can" but "won't"?

   - When reprimanding someone, do you reaffirm the person's past performance at the end?

5. Avoid no response.

   Strength _____ Needs improvement _____

   - Could you be accused of not noticing the performance of your people?

- Have you ever "seagulled" in on your people—swooped in, made a lot of noise, dumped on everyone, and then flown away somewhere?

HONESTY-BASED

1. Have integrity.

   Strength _____ Needs improvement _____

   - Would others consider you a moral person?

   - How do you keep things in perspective?

   - Are you impatient? Do you want what you want right now? Or do you trust that things will work out?

   - How do you model integrity for your team? Do you think integrity pays—that you don't have to cheat to win?

2. Show congruence.

   Strength _____ Needs improvement _____

   - Are you congruent? Do you do what you say you're going to do?

- Do you have the trust and confidence of the people you coach?

- To what extent do you feel that your performers are honest with you?

- Do you walk your talk?

3. Have a sense of humor.

   Strength _____ Needs improvement _____

   - How important is humor in your coaching?

   - Are you ever the target of humor? Are you able to laugh at yourself?

   - Do you take what you do seriously but yourself lightly?

Good luck! The coaching secrets you have learned in this book have held up for over three decades. We hope they will help you to be better tomorrow than today, better next week than last week, better next month than last month, better next year than last year. Remember, coaching is one of the most important roles you can ever have. Helping others to be their best is a great opportunity. Do it well!

ABOUT
THE AUTHORS

■ *Don Shula* is pro football's winningest coach and was selected as 1993 Sportsman of the Year by *Sports Illustrated.* His accomplishments reached a peak on November 14, 1993, when the Miami Dolphins defeated the Philadelphia Eagles 19–14. Shula won his 325th career game that afternoon and became the winningest coach in NFL history, surpassing George Halas' career total of 324 victories, a feat once thought to be impossible.

Some of the stops along this journey have established victory and championship yardsticks virtually unmatched in NFL history:

- Shula is the only coach to guide a team (the Miami Dolphins) through an undefeated season (17–0 in 1972).

- Shula has appeared in six Super Bowls, more than any other coach.

- Since 1970 Shula led the Dolphins to the best regular-season winning percentage of any team in professional sports.

- Shula has amassed 319 regular season wins in his thirty-two years as a head coach, just one win short of averaging ten wins per season.

- Shula is the youngest coach to win 100 games.

- Shula is the youngest coach to win 200 games.

- Shula is the youngest coach to win 300 games.

Shula especially values his family life and his Catholic faith. He was married to the former Dorothy Bartish for over thirty-two years before she passed away in 1991. They raised five children—two boys and three girls. Oldest son David is the head coach of the Cincinnati Bengals. Younger son Mike is the tight end coach of the Chicago Bears. Shula and his wife, Mary Anne, whom he married on October 16, 1993, reside in Miami.

■ *Ken Blanchard* is an internationally known author, educator, and consultant trainer. His *One Minute Manager Library,* coauthored with some of America's best thinkers, has sold more than nine million copies and has been translated into more than twenty-five languages. He has also written or coauthored four other books, including *The Power of Ethical Management* with Norman Vincent Peale and *Raving Fans,* coauthored with Sheldon Bowles. His most recent book, *We Are the Beloved,* chronicles his spiritual journey.

Blanchard has received a multitude of awards in management and leadership. In 1991 he received the National Speakers' Association's highest honor, the Council of Peers Award for Excellence, and in 1992 he was inducted into the Human Resources Development Hall of Fame by *Training Magazine* and Lakewood Conferences. Also in 1992 he received the Golden Gavel from Toastmasters International.

In 1979 Blanchard cofounded Blanchard Training and Development, Inc. (BTD), headquartered in Escondido, California, with his wife, Marjorie. The Blanchards, both graduates of Cornell University, and their associates consult with and teach leaders and managers throughout the world about how to be better coaches and create empowered organizations. A partial client list includes Disney, Glaxo, Honda, Kodak, Lenscrafters, Petro Canada, and The Gap.

The Blanchards have two children, Scott and Debbie, both of whom work for BTD. Debbie is in marketing communications, and Scott is in the training and consulting area. All the Blanchards reside in San Diego.

SERVICES AVAILABLE

Don Shula and Ken Blanchard are available to speak to conventions and organizations on the C.O.A.C.H. concepts. In addition, these concepts can be brought alive in your organization and personal life through audiotapes and videotapes. A special seminar and implementation planner has been jointly developed by Blanchard Training and Development, Inc. (BTD) and Franklin Quest, the originator of the Franklin Planner System. For information on these products and programs, or if you have any questions about *Everyone's a Coach* or about Ken Blanchard's availability, contact:

Blanchard Training and Development, Inc.
125 State Place
Escondido, CA 92029
619 489-5005
800 728-6000
Attention: Harry Paul or Pete Psichogios

BTD also provides in-depth consulting and seminars in all areas of organizational service and performance.

For further information on Don Shula's availability or if you have questions about *Everyone's a Coach,* contact:

Charles O. Morgan, Jr., PA
1300 Northwest 167th Street
Miami, FL 33169
305 624-0011